THREE LIONS
ON HER SHIRT

THREE LIONS
ON HER SHIRT

The England Women's Story

Catherine Etoe and **Natalia Sollohub**

To Louisa, Tim, Harry, Ned and Eric

First published 2007

STADIA is an imprint of
Tempus Publishing Ltd
Cirencester Road, Chalford,
Stroud, Gloucestershire GL6 8PE
www.tempus-publishing.com

British Library Cataloguing in Publication Data.
A catalogue record for this book is available from the British Library.

ISBN 978 0 7524 4448 2

Typesetting and origination by NPI Media Group
Printed in Great Britain

Contents

About the Authors

Catherine Etoe is a writer and photographer who has had work published by *The Guardian*, *Daily Telegraph*, Professional Footballers' Association website givemefootball.com, *Fair Game* magazine, TheFA.com and London weekly papers *The Islington Tribune* and *Camden New Journal*. She captained Blackpool Ladies FC in the early 1990s and currently plays five-a-side football with the Flying Elephants in London. She could never have played for England. At any level.

Natalia Sollohub has been involved in football all her life in a variety of ways: as a player, spectator, researcher and photographer to name a few. After finally finding a team to play for during her university years, she can count a five-minute appearance for Scottish Universities as her only international experience. Neither England nor Russia came calling, however, and she has since worked as a football highlights editor for live television as well as regularly contributing to women's football magazine *Fair Game* for many years.

Acknowledgements

The authors would like to thank the entire England squad and management for taking the time to share their lives and experiences with us. We are also grateful for the valuable insights from the following: Vic Akers, Sheila Aluko, Tina Asante, Marcus Bignot, Keith Boanas, John Buckley, Karen Burke, Marie Carney, Ted Copeland, Gill Coultard, Louise Edwards, Albert Fellowes, Jim Hicks, Nigel Hyde, Gill Jones, John Jones, Mo Marley, Carol McKee, Frank McMorrow, Wendy Owen, Vera Pauw, Eartha Pond, Martin Reagan, Steve Shipway, Ann and Syd Smith, Bernard Smith, Marieanne Spacey, Phil and Sandra Stoney, Terry Unitt, Lou Waller, Clare Wheatley, Trevor White, Linda Whitehead, Mark Wilkinson and Harvey Chapman, and Jean Yankey. Thanks for assistance in a variety of ways must also go to Deb Browne, David Barber, Clare, Ewan and James Campbell, Gavin Ellis, Kelly MacMillan, Martin Newman, Jen O'Neill, Rachel Pavlou, Gavin Peacock, Helen Reagan, Maria Sollohub, Andy Spence, Alex Stone, Mel Vauvelle, Katie Willis and Phil Worrall. We would like to thank Rob Sharman, Lucy Chowns, Jill Ord and all involved at Tempus Publishing for their assistance. Special thanks for all their love and support go to Louisa Tamplin, Adam Townsend, Jill Etoe, Tim Hayward and Valerie Sollohub.

In at the Deep End

Only one thing beats playing football for your country, and that is playing football for your country in the biggest competition on the planet – the World Cup. The trick is getting there. It is a job that takes a year of hard graft, a dash of luck, canny management and a burning hunger. England had those ingredients in spades when they embarked on their bid to make it to the 2007 World Cup in China. Over the years, the women who made up the squad had pulled off *Bend It Like Beckham*-style excuses, juggled intensive training schedules with their daily grind, survived the kind of injuries that would have seen most players quit the sport forever and pretended to be boys – just to carry on playing the game they had grown to love.

The England Lionesses would need all their reserves of strength and guile to make it through this particular attempt to land a place among the world elite. A few months earlier, an expectant England had crashed out of the European Championship on home soil. Finishing bottom of their Euro 2005 group was gut wrenching, especially after manager Hope Powell's young team had captured the imagination of the nation with a last-gasp win over Finland as a modern-day record crowd of 29,092 roared them on at the City of Manchester Stadium in their opening match. Six days and two games later, England were out of the tournament and had to content themselves with a view from the stands as Germany powered their way to the trophy yet again, this time with an emphatic 3-1 final-day win over Norway on a rainy afternoon in Blackburn. Powell was there, but mentally she had already moved on, preoccupied with thoughts of World Cup qualification. Later that summer, as she gathered her squad around her for the first time since those frustrating Euro days, she was adamant that they would do the same.

'Hope said, "You won't think it now but you'll learn so much from this and it will help you improve," and it's done exactly that, we've found qualities that we didn't know we had,' says England no.1 Rachel Brown, looking back to their team briefing after Euro 2005 had ended. Still only twenty-four during the tournament, Brown was already a veteran of the England set-up, called up in the days when manager Ted Copeland ran the show and was giving promising teenagers like Mary Phillip, Sue Smith, Faye White, Kelly Smith and Rachels Yankey and Brown a chance in the seniors. Copeland recalls:

> In the early days I spent a lot of time watching players up and down the country... But I found that the best way to see if talented players could move up to a higher level and handle the pressures of international football was to bring them into the squad and see if they could adapt.

The then rookies did just that and are the lynchpins of former England midfielder Hope Powell's squad today. But much has changed since she swapped her place as their teammate for the role as their international manager.

To do so, Powell had to fill the shoes of the man who had given those youngsters a chance but had kept her sitting on the bench for part of the 1995 World Cup. Ted Copeland took over the England reins back in 1993, the same year that the Football Association finally took charge of the women's game. Qualification for the World Cup was markedly different then. To reach the 2007 World Cup, England were battling with four other nations – two ranked in the top twenty in the world – for one European slot. Back then, England's qualification was dependent on a good showing in the European Championship: Copeland's side lost to Germany in a two-legged semi-final but it was enough to stake a place in the twelve-nation World Cup 1995 that June. Out in Sweden, England edged a five-goal thriller against Canada 3-2, stumbled to Norway 2-0 but beat Nigeria 3-2 to make the quarter-finals, where they lost, again, to Germany. Powell came off the bench in three of those games as Copeland tried out squad rotation to keep his side fresh, but she admits she did not enjoy kicking her heels:

> I didn't like being on the bench. No disrespect to Ted, he had a type of player and I wasn't it... Did I play? Yes. Did I play as often as I would have liked? Probably not. I had lots of conversations with him after that World Cup about the way we played and the type of player I was.

It was a different story when Powell first teamed up with England as a sixteen-year-old. The manager back in 1983 was Martin Reagan, a former professional footballer with Middlesbrough and Portsmouth, among others. The Geordie set up regional teams to help him assess the best players from across the country and, once he had found them, used circuit training to get his England amateurs fit. Now in his eighties, Reagan's failing eyesight has forced him to hang up his tracksuit after fifty years as a coach. But he is still involved in grass-roots football as vice president of the York Minor League and can still vividly recall the day he called up the woman who would eventually pick up his mantle. 'She was a Rolls Royce of a player,' recalls Reagan. 'She had everything, you could hardly find a flaw in her and the response when she first joined the squad was all the players saying, "Where did you find her?".'

Reagan had found Powell at Millwall Lionesses, the club the Peckham-raised youngster initially pretended not to have joined to placate her worried mother. 'I grew up playing on the street, finding that you were as good as, if not better than the boys and thinking that you are the only girl who plays football,' she recalls. A school friend told Powell otherwise and invited her to Millwall. Having been stopped from turning out for her secondary-school team by a mixed football age ban, Powell took up her friend's offer and one training session with the Lionesses later, the eleven-year-old was being asked to sign up:

> I was really surprised at how many girls played football... They asked me to come back but I got home very late that night and my mum said, 'You are not going again'. Come Sunday I went, said I'd gone to the chip shop or something. I was that girl in *Bend It Like Beckham*, in part.

Luckily for Powell, mum soon came round to the idea so the new Millwall reservist did not have to make up far-fetched excuses every Sunday afternoon. The youngster did have to make up her mind as to where her future lay, though, when she was asked to wave farewell to her mates in the reserves and move into the senior side. 'I said no at first but then I realised that you need to play for the first team,' she shrugs.

Powell was less backwards in coming forwards the minute she found out there was an England first team, recalling how she remarked to one club colleague, 'I will play for England one day.' There was a less assured reaction when the shy teenager finally pulled on the England kit at a training camp. 'I was thrown into this big world of grown-up women's football,' she says. 'I was at school and they all had cars.' Powell says that without the camaraderie of teammates Brenda Sempare and Angela Gallimore, she might have struggled to adapt. 'I was this kid and had I not been with Brenda and Angela, would I have survived it? Would I have found it pleasurable? I don't know,' she shrugs. But survive she did and Powell became the first Millwall Lioness to represent her country when she took to the field at Reading FC in a European qualifier against the Republic of Ireland. England trounced the visitors 6-0 and their most successful international period to date was underway.

Under Reagan the national side made the final of the inaugural European Championship, losing in a cruel penalty shoot-out after beating Sweden at Luton in the home tie of the two-legged final in 1984.

They tasted more success in Italy than rain-sodden Luton, lifting the 'mini World Cup', the Mundialito, in 1985, and being showered with flowers during a standing ovation from the Italy fans, despite being an English team arriving in the country so soon after the Heysel disaster in which Juventus fans had died. 'It was quite a poignant moment,' recalls Gill Coultard, England's most capped outfield player, male or female. Reagan's team repeated their Mundialito cup-winning trick three years later. They were noteworthy achievements made in a time when the Women's Football Association was running the national team on a shoestring, when Reagan was part-time and had no proper back-room staff, when England had one kit and a sense of togetherness was crucial. Former WFA secretary Linda Whitehead recalls:

> It was fun but everything was difficult because we had very little funding and were underdogs wherever we went. But one of the things that brought us through was that team spirit and that was down to Martin Reagan because he made everybody believe that they were all special and we all played for one another.

Team spirit alone could not stop England from being left behind in the international pecking order, however. The WFA had been set up in 1969 while the men's World Cup victory was still fresh in the nation's mind. Two years later, the 1921 ban on women playing on grounds belonging to clubs associated to the FA was lifted, and by 1972 the first England women's team was in place. But as time went on, the WFA's national team found itself at a distinct disadvantage to countries that had been supported by their national associations since the 1970s. 'When I went to other countries it really opened your eyes,' says Reagan. 'They had the money and facilities and backing of their national FAs and sponsorship.' That backing arrived for the England women in 1993; two years after Reagan's reign had ended with a creditable record of 37 wins and 14 draws in 70 games. Ted Copeland eventually took on the part-time job that year, combining it with his existing role as regional director of coaching for the North at the FA for a good five years. Within two years of his appointment, Copeland had taken England to an impressive semi-final berth in the European Championship and to the last eight of the World Cup.

But if silverware was not forthcoming, changes were. Coming under the umbrella of the FA, England women suddenly found themselves enjoying the same kit sponsorship as the men. 'We were just shocked that we were given these things by Umbro and everybody was asking, "Do we have to give them back?"' recalls World Cup 1995 striker Marieanne Spacey. It was quite a turnaround given that in the previous decade they had gratefully accepted training kit donations from the Swedish team. 'When they came and said "Do you want one of these?" you snapped their hands off,' laughs her old colleague Coultard. Indeed, even washing what kit the squad had came down to WFA stalwarts like Linda Whitehead and the late Flo Bilton, the players – and their mums. 'My mum washed the kit at my nan's house and the neighbours were all coming in looking at the England kit on the washing line,' recalls Spacey of wash day during a tournament in Ireland.

But it was not just the shirts and socks the England players wore that had changed; more importantly, two international youth sides were set up in 1997 and 1998 and backing was given to new centres of excellence across the country. From then on, promising schoolgirls, like Spacey and Powell had been, would no longer be thrown in at the deep end when it came to playing for England. Spearheading those changes, which were all part of the FA's 1997 Talent Development Plan for women's football, were the then FA technical director Howard Wilkinson, the FA's women's football co-ordinator Kelly Simmons, Ted Copeland and, a year later, their new full-time England managerial appointee Hope Powell.

Former England midfielder Powell had enjoyed a glittering career that had seen her amass 66 caps and 35 goals internationally alongside two FA Cups domestically, the last of which was secured with double winners Croydon against Rachel Brown's Liverpool in 1996.

Within a couple of years of that victory, Croydon captain Powell had started to look to life beyond her playing days and applied for one of the FA's regional development jobs. The midfielder had taken her first coaching badge aged eighteen and had made her living in sports development for Crystal Palace FC and Lewisham Council, so it seemed a good way to remain in the game. Firing off her CV to the FA's old headquarters in Lancaster Gate brought more than England's vice-captain had bargained for, however:

> I just wanted to work in football so I just went for this job at the FA and thought my credentials might swing it a bit… I got called back and thought it was something to do with the Under-18s and when they told me I was very cool.

With Ted Copeland having resigned as manager for personal reasons, what the FA had told Powell was that they wanted her to become the country's first full-time, first female and youngest ever England women's team coach. To sway her decision, they spent a week introducing Powell to the powers that be at FA headquarters and even showed her around then England men's manager Glenn Hoddle's office.

> I was, oh okay, well I need time to decide. Then I walked out and I was, oh my god. Went to a friend's because my partner wasn't home and I had to tell somebody and said, 'What do you think? I don't know if I should take it,' and they said, 'Are you mad? You've got to.'

Powell remained unsure, however, until Kelly Simmons chipped in with a few choice words of wisdom. 'She said to me, "You know what Hope, if you don't take it you will be sitting in the changing rooms as a player thinking I could have done this",' Powell says. 'And I thought, why not? I've got nothing to lose.'

There was no time to waste either as Powell took over from caretaker-manager Dick Bate. A friendly against Sweden was looming and there were the new Under-16 and Under-18 sides to get to grips with. In the meantime, Powell set about assessing everything she had liked and disliked as an England player. It was quite a list. 'It is easier to say what I didn't like,' she shrugs in her neat and compact office in the FA's Soho Square headquarters:

> I didn't like the fact that we didn't play very often, we were not together as a squad enough, we didn't have the opportunity to get the players in outside of playing a match, we weren't fit enough, we would lose games in the last ten minutes, probably didn't have the support, the medical support was not what it should be – it was all the little things that make a massive difference.

Luckily, former Sheffield Wednesday and Leeds United boss Howard Wilkinson's open-door policy towards Powell allowed her to turn those gripes into something more positive:

> He was so supportive and if it was not for him I don't know. He respected the fact that he was not the expert in women's football and used to say, 'Tell me what you need and I'll get it for you' and today we have got most things, nearly everything that I wanted.

That shopping list of 'must-haves' was written over the next few years as Powell explored the international set-ups of Germany, Sweden and the US, rivals who were prepared to become allies when it came to the swapping of ideas. Powell says:

> We've had lots of discussions with them about what they do and the beauty of women's football is that everyone is happy to share... We had a coaches forum in Switzerland and everyone is quite open about what they are doing. You sometimes want to know if you're doing the right thing.

The right thing that was decided upon for England included: an Under-21 side to bridge the gap between the seniors and Under-19s (formerly the Under-18s); an Under-15 development

Hope Powell sets her sights on World Cup qualification.

squad for those too young for the Under-17s (the old Under-16s); and an FA-funded football centre for twenty elite players who want to combine education and football. All of which, along with centres of excellence and academies, created a ladder for the most talented players to clamber their way up.

In 2005, as she looked at her squad list for England's World Cup 2007 qualifying matches, Powell knew she had already reaped the rewards of that player pathway, even if easing up-and-coming players in ahead of former teammates had been a tricky task. Powell admits:

> That was probably the most difficult thing I had to do. You don't want to upset players but my job is not to be liked, my job is to try and get the best out of what we've got. One of the things I thought was, we are an older team and in five years it's going to be struggling. As a result you end up changing things round and picking other players.

Among those elevated by Powell to senior status were Katie Chapman, Rachel Unitt, Fara Williams, Karen Carney, Eniola Aluko, Alex Scott and Anita Asante, all of them having served their England apprenticeships at higher tempos than the occasional friendly, thanks to the increasing numbers of UEFA international youth tournaments. 'From the Under-17s you play the same formation,' says England's Kelly Smith. 'They know the structure of how the first team plays and they know the way the set-up is run. Now, they have more knowledge coming up whereas I was sixteen and came into the full women's team and didn't know anything.'

Come 2005, Powell was also benefiting from the move away from the one man and his dog approach to the England women's team. There was a time when England's manager merely had to ask a part-time physiotherapist to shove up if he wanted a seat on the bench. Today, Powell has to jostle with a doctor, physiotherapist, performance analyst, goalkeeping coach, nutritionist, exercise scientist, video technician and psychologist if she wants to take a pew. Not that Powell is complaining – most of those bench-hogging colleagues were brought in at her behest in the months that followed England's failure to make the 2003 World Cup. France were the bogey side that time round, beating England on home soil at Crystal Palace's Selhurst Park and again in St Etienne to take the fifth European qualification spot. Over in France, a crowd of over 23,000 baying fans cheered their side's victory while a dejected England fell sobbing to the turf, their bid to make the biggest competition in women's football in tatters. Undeterred, Powell looked to innovations in the men's game to beef up her team both physically and mentally. 'We introduced new things,' she says. 'Brought in a psychologist, brought in extra conditioning staff, technical strategy – changed that slightly – you know, made subtle changes that I knew would have an impact over time.' As the 2007 World Cup loomed, the time to put those changes to the test had arrived.

Where's Wongy?

Barely two months after the disappointment of Euro 2005, the squad were back together to prepare for the all-important year-long assault on World Cup qualification. There was plenty of news to catch up on as the tight-knit Euro group, alongside eight recalled players, gathered at the Lilleshall National Sports Centre in Shropshire. Right-back Alex Scott, defender Casey Stoney, winger Jo Potter and midfielder Anita Asante had enjoyed a successful post-Euro summer helping the Under-21s to a highly respectable third place in the Nordic Cup in Sweden. While Eni Aluko and Karen Carney, the teenagers who had captured the nation's hearts and the media's imagination during the Euros, had given the Under-19s a leg-up. Less than a month after the senior tournament ended in Lancashire, the two had flown to Hungary to play for the Under-19s in their own version of the competition. Senior keeper Rachel Brown was on hand to act as a goalkeeping coach and despite being familiar faces to the youth squad, the trio's Euro 2005 experiences brought a dash of star quality to coach Mo Marley's line-up. But even Brown, Aluko and Carney could not inspire England's youngsters to anything higher than a sixth-placed finish, a lowly position that dashed dreams of a place in the forthcoming Under-20 World Cup. Elsewhere, though, Rachels Unitt and Yankey had tasted success. The two jetted out to America to play for the New Jersey Wildcats alongside the likes of US international Heather O'Reilly, and between them they helped the East Coast club bag the prestigious W-League championship trophy for the first time in their ten-year history.

Regardless of their respective summertime antics, the Euros still dominated catch-up chat – even with those who had missed out on selection. For England regular and team prankster Sue 'Wongy' Smith, who had not made the cut for the Euros, being back in the loop again was a strange experience. 'It was a bit weird because I'd been in it for so long, the girls were like, "Do you remember when that happened in the Euros?" and I was, "Well no," and they would say, "I'm so sorry",' she recalls. It was an understandable lapse. One major injury aside, the cheery Merseysider had rarely missed an England meet since announcing her arrival on the international scene eight and a half years earlier alongside fellow rookie, goal-keeper Rachel Brown. Smith was just seventeen when she replaced an injured Kelly Smith that chilly February night in Preston against Germany. 'She couldn't get on quick enough and was going on with her training coat on but I think I was more nervous than her,' her mum Ann recalls. Smith was not completely calm, however, and admits she ran around Deepdale like a child chasing a party balloon at her own birthday bash. A quiet word in her ear from teammate Hope Powell settled the teenager, though, and by full time she had plundered a goal against the reigning European champions. 'Hope helped me,' she says. 'I was like a young kid running everywhere and she was just like, "calm down".' That goal, alongside a penalty from Powell and a brace from Jo Broadhurst, helped England claw back a humbling 5-0 deficit to a more respectable 6-4, much to the relief of the fans and Smith's parents. Mum Ann says, 'After that the crowd were behind her, they were shouting "Give it to the winger".'

Crowds in the north-west were denied the chance to make that call of encouragement during the Euros. Despite figuring and scoring in the Algarve Cup friendly tournament in Portugal just three months earlier, and appearing in pre-tournament publicity – including Blackburn's Christmas lights switch on with pop hunk Peter Andre – the local lass with the tufty blonde mop and pointy pigtails was not among the final twenty names read out by England boss Powell to the waiting media in Soho Square in May 2005. 'I think

The Euro 2005 fans want Sue Smith on the pitch, not in the studio.

she would admit she wasn't in the best form of her life,' says Smith's England colleague Brown. 'She was coming back from a long-term injury and was not quite as strong as she had been.' Even so, their bubbly colleague's absence was felt when the team gathered together for the tournament. 'It was weird, it felt like there was someone missing,' says Rachel Unitt. 'Wongy is a great person to have within the camp. She's a character and she makes everyone laugh.' It did not stop her northern following from chipping in with their opinion on the decision either. Banners declaring 'Bring Back Sue Smith' were flaunted at Blackburn Rovers' Ewood Park ground during England's Euro games.

But Powell's decision was final, so instead of playing a good game for her country, Smith spent the tournament talking one to the country as a Euro 2005 analyst for the BBC. 'I was really gutted but then I got a phone call from the BBC,' she says. 'I had thought about going away but doing the BBC was good. I just blocked out that I wasn't playing and just focused on getting behind them through the TV.' Rehearsing opposition players' names with her mum in Hyde

Park so as not to 'sound like a div' on the telly, and throwing her twopenn'orth of opinion in on the performances of her peers while sitting on the BBC's big orange sofa with ex-Chelsea star Gavin Peacock was fun, Smith admits. It had to be if it was going to make up for what she describes as the biggest disappointment of her footballing life.

That life began more than two decades earlier while watching older brother Carl play in the field close to the house in Merseyside that Smith still calls home. The affable Scouser's hair was less flamboyant in those days and she had yet to acquire her football nickname Wongy (named after a cat owned by former Tranmere and later Leeds teammate Natalie Preston). But Smith's ability with a football was there for all to see while she was just a toddler. 'Even when she was in her pram she never threw a ball, always kicked it,' recall Ann and Syd Smith. Sitting in the front room of a home dotted with their daughter's team photos and trophies, Ann laughs, 'I tried her with the dancing and took her to all the things that little girls do, even joined her in the Brownies, but she came home and said, "It's sewing all the time, I'd rather play football."'

Luckily, Carl's club were willing to take Smith on and the eight-year-old football fanatic ran out for the boys of Rainhill United where she quickly grabbed the goals – and the headlines. 'Her skill and determination with the ball is as good as any boy her own age and older,' rang out one glowing club report in the local newspaper. Indeed, coach Albert Fellowes was so impressed with the player that he made Smith his captain and predicted she would run out for England one day. 'At that stage I thought I'd be playing for England men,' Smith smirks. 'I didn't know there was a women's team.' Just a few years later, Smith rewarded Fellowes' belief in her by presenting him with the England (women's) shirt she had donned on her debut. 'She was true to her word,' says Fellowes, who now has the shirt displayed proudly in a wooden frame.

Not everyone was as enthusiastic as Rainhill when it came to girls playing in a boys' world though. Smith found school teams were off limits because of fears for her safety and parents' complaints that the lads would not dare tackle a lass. Whether the boys themselves saw it that way, Smith's mum is not so sure. 'Most of the lads she'd grown up with so she expected to tackle them and they would tackle her,' she shrugs. The happy-go-lucky pupil's matches with her boys' team also came to an end when mixed-team age-limit rules kicked in while she was still at primary school. Her manager Albert Fellowes, a distinguished coach who was honoured with an MBE in the Queen's Birthday Honours List 2003 for his services to the Rainhill community, knew he was losing a key player. 'The lads all wanted to be on her side,' he recalls. 'Normally girls are good at a girl's level but she was good at any level.' It was a decision that caused consternation within the club, with the coach telling the local paper at the time:

> It is ironic that when we have training all the boys want her to be on their side because she is that good... The rules say that she can't play and so that is it. But at our presentation evening we awarded Sue a special trophy for her outstanding performances last season.

Smith is not the only player in England's ranks to have been hit by mixed-team diktats as a child. Hope Powell still has the newspaper cuttings dating back to the days when she was told she could not play for her secondary school team in Peckham. 'The school made a big deal about it at the time,' Powell recalls. 'I just wanted to play like every other kid.' It was a difficult task in an era of few girls' teams. 'Any one of the squad over twenty-five says the same thing: there were hardly any teams,' says the FA's press manager Alex Stone. 'Now it's on the curriculum.' On the syllabus it may be, but a 2006 House of Commons Select Committee on women's football found that of all the countries with mixed-football age limits, England's cut-off when girls turn eleven is among the lowest. The reasoning behind the rule is safety, but campaigning body the Women's Sports Foundation told the committee it was an 'artificial barrier' and the age limit should be based on weight, height and ability instead of age. Wendy Owen, who ran out for the first official England team in 1972, agrees. The UEFA 'B' coaching licence holder says that since she published her autobiography *Kicking Against Tradition* concerned parents have written to her about their girls being forced to quit their mixed teams. In a memorandum submitted to the Select Committee, Owen, a coach of more than thirty years' standing, states, 'With girls maturing earlier on average than boys, they are often physically capable of playing mixed football well beyond the age of eleven. Matching children for height, weight and ability may be a better way of organising sport competition.'

The issue was due to be discussed by world football's governing body FIFA at their women's committee ahead of the 2007 World Cup. The FA's courting of opinion via a 'Your Game Your Say' website questionnaire, a survey of around 5,000 under-sixteen girls and research at centres of excellence had so far proved inconclusive come spring 2007, although there was 'low appeal' for integrated teams from both sexes. It is a contrast to attitudes in Holland, one of the countries the FA has been looking to in its research. There, girls can play football with their male counterparts until they are nineteen. Dutch national team manager Vera Pauw, a triplet who kicked a football with her brothers until her late teens, says it is a 'crucial' structure that has been gradually introduced:

> At youth level it was normal for a six-year-old girl to play with a fourteen-year-old girl because she had a ponytail and no-one was saying this is not our standard. I knew from my toes that girls and boys can play together because I've done that on the streets until I was eighteen or nineteen. I was very much convinced that that was the way to go and from the moment we changed the rules, in one year the number of girls playing football doubled and now it's common practice.

In England, Smith is a prime example of the benefits of continuing to play alongside boys. Like Powell and others who were affected by the rules over the years, Smith was determined to keep pulling on those footy boots despite her ban. So at the tender age of nine, the player negotiated a move to nearby St Helens Ladies FC and sorted out training sessions at their boys' school of excellence. It was a time when girls' centres of excellence were still some way off, but it was to prove an invaluable double whammy. Looking back, Smith says, 'I learnt a lot from them because it's a different game from the girls' game and that stood me in good stead.' The sports-mad youngster kept up a hectic timetable during her school days, receiving a call-up from, of all things, the England Under-21 rounders team, while throwing herself into hockey, netball and her other big passion, tennis. Running around with racquet and ball in hand was a definite contrast to kicking a football around a pitch, but Smith reasoned it had never done the man whose posters adorned her bedroom walls any harm. 'Gazza was my childhood hero and he was a tennis player so whether that had anything to do with it I don't know,' she laughs.

Football was still Smith's first love, though, and by the time she was fourteen, the Paul Gascoigne fan was looking to play at an even higher level. Teaming up with nearby Tranmere Rovers threw Smith into North West Regional League action, but not for long. Tranmere's star rose as fast as their energetic midfielder's was about to and in the mid-1990s the Merseysiders were elevated to the National Division after marching off with consecutive League titles. The club's elevation to the shop window of the Premier League proved a turning point for their home-loving prospect Smith. England came calling that first top-flight season, much to the delight of her neighbours and friends. 'There was such excitement waiting to see whether she got picked,' says Ann Smith, who recalls a stream of inquisitive callers popping their heads around the door of the flower shop she worked in demanding to know if their girl would make her debut. A sixteen-year-old Smith had to watch from the Prenton Park stands when she failed to make the cut in her first England call-up, an unlucky 1-1 draw against Spain at nearby Tranmere Rovers FC. It was a different story five months later when Germany paid a visit to Preston. 'Sue was one of a number of exciting young players who appeared at the time and had great technical ability,' recalls her former England manager Ted Copeland. So it would seem, with Smith coming off the bench to grab a goal – and a taste of fame. 'You were a little celeb in school and they would make a big deal of it in assemblies,' Smith recalls. 'It was a bit surreal, at that age, I just used to go and play and didn't really think much of it and people just accepted that I was playing for England.'

Playing was exactly what the life-long Evertonian kept on doing after that debut goal against a merciless Germany side when she was seventeen. But if that performance against the powerhouse of European football had the teenager knocking at the international door, she had the key to it firmly in her pocket by February 1999. Smith readily admits to sporting an almost geriatric memory when it comes to matches or key moments in games. But leaning back in a broad armchair with the family's Jack Russell hyperactively brushing up against her ankles, she enthusiastically recalls her selection as the nation's only representative in the prestigious FIFA World Stars XI for a match against World Cup 1999 hosts USA. Hoping to avoid wind-ups from her Tranmere teammates, Smith kept the news hush hush, thinking she could nip off to America for the weekend and return without the team even noticing. 'I didn't tell anyone because the girls at Tranmere were the ones that kept my feet on the ground and would be just like "So!"' she laughs. The girls got wind of the selection, though. Former Tranmere defender Louise Edwards remembers being incredulous that their teammate had not shared the news. 'We did take the mick because she was like a super star even though she wasn't big-headed,' recalls Edwards, who went on to manage the first team. 'But when we found out we were all made up for her, it was the biggest thing anyone had ever done from our club and we were proud of her.' Today, Smith is less reticent about proclaiming such a remarkable call-up and takes the shirt she wore in that World Cup 1999 exhibition match around schools as part of her work for Sporting Champions. 'I really should put it in a frame,' she laughs, eyeing the blue no.18

Syd Smith proudly dons one of daughter Sue's international caps.

shirt for grubby schoolboy and girl handprints. But the personal touch and ethos of Sporting Champions, a scheme funded by Sport England and designed to get youngsters into sport by letting them meet players and athletes, is what grabs Smith. Perhaps because her mum still reminds her of the day she returned home from a football festival a year before her England bow, all wide-eyed and excited after speaking to two of the national team's players – one of whom would become a Leeds teammate. 'I remember her coming home and saying, "I spoke to Karen Burke" and she was delighted,' laughs Ann Smith, much to her daughter's embarrassment now that she and former England midfielder Burkey, capped 69 times for her country, are club colleagues.

Smith played the first half of that game against the US, being replaced by Australia's Julie Murray as a World Stars side came back from 1-0 down to beat Mia Hamm and Co. 2-1 in front of over 15,000 excited fans in the Spartan Stadium in San Jose, California. But the appearance did not just serve to bolster the 'achievements' section on Smith's CV. The entire experience made a star-struck Smith yearn to handle the media with as much composure as her American counterparts. Watching the US's face of football Mia Hamm field questions from reporters with all the aplomb of an experienced politician was an inspiration for a player who would later make ends meet partly through her television punditry:

> We were doing press conferences and it was just like the men, there were all the different TV stations and we were just like, wow… I remember listening to the Americans and how good they were at dealing with the media. It was all a bit surreal but something I'll never forget.

Hot on the heels of that game against the glamorous Americans, Smith flirted with a dash of star treatment herself. Having picked up an FA International Player of the Year award and National Division Players' Player of the Year award in 1999 she was later treated to a makeover by women's magazine, and then Tranmere shirt sponsors, *Chat*. It was a revamp that saw the England no.11 ditch the bushy longhaired schoolgirl look for a trendier, shorter and spikier cut. It was a look Smith was to later restyle into a chichi hairdo that was all her own. But it was not the flair of her hair that drew the fans to the player; it was the flair of her football. Still flying high with England come November 2000, Smith's goal alongside one from Rachel Yankey against the Ukraine at Leyton Orient secured England's place in Euro 2001.

By the time Smith flew with her international colleagues to the tournament in Germany, she had netted a hat-trick in a 4-2 conquest of Spain at Luton, picked up a second International Player of the Year award and her England tally was a whacking 32 caps and 11

A post-makeover Sue Smith (11) lines up alongside Kirsty Pealling (2), Faye White (5) and Rachel Yankey (10) for a friendly against Denmark straight after Euro 2001.

goals. She racked up three more caps in that well-attended competition. But emerging from a 'group of death' that featured eventual finalists Germany and Sweden was beyond England and they were unable to progress to the latter stages of a tournament that attracted a then record total of 94,648 spectators. With World Cup 2003 qualifiers pencilled in to the diary less than three months later, the time for England to make amends followed swiftly. Smith would only play her part in two of them. The winger's rising star came crashing down one Friday night in February 2002 when she suffered a painful leg break during a friendly game of five-a-side with a bunch of local lads. 'It was a freak,' Smith recalls. 'I took a shot and the ball rebounded and I landed on it. No tackle, no impact.' Smith had dislocated her ankle and broken her leg. Just a few months later, the player was frantically dialling the number of then England physiotherapist Louise Fawcett insisting she was up and running again. Unfortunately for Smith, by the time the physiotherapist had given her the thumbs up fitness wise ahead of the World Cup 2003 play-offs, the squad's other joker in the pack, Rachel Yankey, was first choice on the left wing. Yankey had played up front for England since her debut in 1997 while a striker with Arsenal. But Fulham boss Frank McMorrow moved the lightening-quick youngster to left wing towards the end of her first season with the Cottagers and the Londoner had made the position her own, as Yankey explains:

> At the beginning, I was playing up front and Sue was playing on the wing and then it came that we were in a rivalry, competing for the same position... But there's never been that rivalry between me and her. Obviously both of us want to play, but we've always been good mates about it.

It was still a difficult demotion for Smith, who had gone straight into the Leeds line-up after signing in the summer of 2002 and had always been one of the first names on the team sheet at her old club Tranmere. She admits:

> I'm the worst sub, probably because before my injury I had never been a sub and at club level I haven't. It's difficult because you are desperate to get on and be a part of it. I don't think I can do a better job; I just think let me on and let me try.

Come the Euros less than three years later, Smith would have taken a seat on the bench just to be involved in a major tournament played in her own back yard, the north-west of England. But her hopes of having done enough to make it at least as back-up for former Fulham and then Birmingham City player Yankey were dashed in a telephone call from England's manager on the eve of the competition. Powell says:

> For Sue it was difficult. You ask her to do anything and she will do it, her attitude is great and for her not to play was devastating and I remember saying, 'You are not picked, these are my reasons but one thing I want you to do is get back to the player you were.'

No hard feelings when best mates Rachel Yankey (left) and Sue Smith celebrate together.

For Smith, the news brought as much heartache as the night she fell over the ball and broke her bones. 'I was gutted and could have said that's it, I don't want to play for England again,' she says. 'But I wanted to play for England so much I just said okay, I'll listen to what Hope has to say. I just want to get into the next training camp.' Tramping up and down the familiar turf of the back field near home and putting in time at a nearby gym in a bid to improve her technique and strength paid off as a delighted Smith was included in the squad set to prepare for a World Cup 2007 qualifying campaign imaginatively dubbed 'China In Your Hands' by the FA.

Two weeks later, England geared up to face Austria in the opening World Cup qualifier. It was the first time in their thirty-three-year history that England had played the Austrians, ranked forty-seventh to their fourteenth, and so Powell's squad went into the match with a clean slate. They also ran out at Ertl Glas Stadion in Amstetten with the disappointment of Euro 2005 well and truly out of their system. 'We thought it was a new chapter and that was said to us: "You've gone through that and new doors are opening",' says midfielder Fara Williams. But while England were looking to move on, Smith appeared to have stood still, because while she was back in the squad, she had fallen even further behind in the pecking order. The fleet-footed Yankey, freshly re-signed to champions Arsenal, was out with an ankle injury. But rather than turn to Smith, Powell opted to give a start to lively Charlton winger and August 2005 League player of the month Jo Potter. Whereas Smith would normally feel heartbroken to be back on the bench, she was simply glad to be back at all. 'I was just happy to be in the squad,' she admits.

And so, as the inaugural match of the campaign kicks off that day in September, Smith can only watch from the sidelines as England fall behind after just twenty minutes, and left-winger Natascha Celouch celebrates with her colleagues after zipping past defender Alex Scott and chipping Rachel Brown from twenty-five yards out. It is a heart stopping moment for the England entourage, especially their keeper. 'It was a really good goal and I don't think anybody including Browny was expecting it,' says Smith. 'I was on the bench and everyone was thinking, "Oh dear, what's going to happen? Are we going to fold?"' But England have more about them than that and a minute later Kelly Smith forces Brown's opposite number Bianca Reischer into a desperate stop in the box. It is a clear penalty and striding up to collect the ball is spot-kick specialist Fara Williams. The midfielder takes a step back, makes a run-up, keeps her eye on the prize and calmly slots the ball beyond the despairing Reischer. England's first goal of the campaign is in the bag and the visitors are back in the match. With their tails up, England are on the attack but Reischer keeps the home side in it when she catches a fifteen-yard cross-shot from striker Amanda Barr, in for the rested Eniola Aluko. But it is not long before the keeper is undone by the irrepressible Kelly Smith once again. Smith unleashes a shot from twenty yards out as England surge forward and though it is a weak effort, Reischer is unable to get to grips with it. England are ahead with just thirty-five minutes played and pretty soon even the defenders are ready to have a go, Rachel Unitt pinging a long shot goalwards just before half-time. Austria survive but go into the break knowing they will need to bounce back if they are to take anything from this match.

Sue Smith's turn to up the tempo finally arrives at the restart. Replacing Potter, the midfielder soon makes an impression, hitting a free-kick that is steered across the box by her old England colleague Kelly Smith and dispatched with aplomb by Barr. England are finally in charge. With Kelly Smith's work done, Hope Powell brings promising midfielder Emily Westwood into the fray. The pressure on Reischer's goal continues to build and it takes a fabulous stop by the keeper to deny Williams' twelve-yard effort seventy-seven minutes in. Austria send out a wake-up call with a minute remaining, Maria Gstöttner threatening with a shot that is kept out by the crossbar. But this is England's day and Sue Smith seals a solid first-game win when she bundles the ball over the line in injury time.

It is scrappy, but 4-1 will do nicely for the team and their veteran winger who can hardly believe how her fortune has changed. 'I was thinking it's quite bizarre that I missed all of the Euros and then first game back I'm in the squad and coming on and scoring a goal,' she shrugs. Smith would go on to suffer the agonies of warming the bench again as the campaign increased in momentum. But her freshly acquired mental toughness would see her through to the final whistle.

Bouncing Back

A trip to Hungary faced England eight weeks after their victory in Austria and three points against the bottom-placed team in the five-nation group would put Hope Powell's side in pole position. Hungary, ranked thirty-first in the world, were winless at this early stage and were not expected to greatly trouble England, seeded seventeen places above them. That did not stop the Hungarian press from harking back to their men's historic win over England in 1953, the days of Stanley Matthews and Ferenc Puskás. Indeed, in the opening paragraph of one match report that followed the game, Hungarian tabloid *Blikk* wrote, 'Fifty-two years ago Hungary taught English football a lesson when we beat them 6-3 at Wembley'. As it turned out, another lesson was doled out in Tapolca. But the woman who helped deliver it was not Hungarian. She was born in Watford.

It was little wonder that Kelly Smith would play such a pivotal role when England travelled to Hungary that month. Widely regarded as the most talented player of her generation, the then twenty-six-year-old had discovered two weeks beforehand that she had made the shortlist of twenty-four nominees for the most coveted award in the game – FIFA Women's World Player of the Year. According to world football's governing body, Smith's inclusion was down to her being 'one of the revelations of the European Championship'. It was quite an achievement given that the player was still suffering the after-effects of a stress fracture to her foot throughout the tournament and spectators in the north-west never really saw the former USA

Kelly Smith finds herself floored with emotion after an England game.

women's league professional in full flight. But 'Kel' had still done enough in the Euros to convince the international captains and managers who voted for the FIFA award that she was among the world's elite. Hungary boss András Telek, fellow nominee and Germany skipper Birgit Prinz and Austria coach Ernst Weber were among those who had inked a cross next to Smith's name. Ironically, the first English player to achieve a FIFA nomination would prove Telek's undoing in Tapolca, 100 miles south-west of Budapest, just as she had Weber's in the opening match only weeks before.

Few at home knew much about England's debut victory over Austria; the national press was more interested in Tunbridge Wells and Littlehampton's new FA Cup penalty record. The Wells edged the mammoth 40-penalty shoot-out contest 16–15 and England's first World Cup qualifying win was consigned to a result in the *Daily Telegraph* and a short report in the *Guardian*. It was a pity for Smith, who had shrugged off her foot injury – and the embarrassment of having to drive a lurid orange car with automatic gears while she recuperated – to show some of the form that justified having her name in the FIFA hat in the first place. The trick now was to stay injury free, a tall order given a track record that included an anterior cruciate ligament tear, torn meniscus, broken leg and fractured foot. They were killer injuries that could have seen off one of the best players in the world – and almost did.

Before her move to professional American side Philadelphia Charge in 2001, the only things Smith had ever picked up in games were bruises and awards. A League Cup trophy win with Wembley was the first piece of silverware Smith got her hands on, followed by a Premier League National Division title with Arsenal, then virtually every honour Seton Hall University on the east coast of America could bestow upon her. In a happy three-year soccer scholarship, the health and physical education major managed to topple a raft of university records including scoring the most game-winning goals, converting the most penalties and even putting away the fastest two goals scored (within eighteen seconds of each other – the keeper did not know what had hit her). They were achievements that earned her the accolade of Rookie of the Year and three Big East Conference Offensive Player of the Year awards. The university even invited her parents Bernard and Carol over to America for a ceremony to make her only the third woman and the first non-basketball-playing female athlete to have her shirt retired. From that day forward, no other footballer at Seton Hall would ever wear the no.6 shirt Smith had been so successful in – that piece of kit sits in a frame at her parents' home in Hertfordshire. The plaudits kept on coming at Smith's next side, W-League club New Jersey Lady Stallions and she was named in the league's all-star team before being picked up in the draft by Philadelphia Charge for the inaugural season of the professional Women's United Soccer Association league. As skipper of the Charge, Smith would experience the joys of leading her team out in stadiums filled with up to 8,000 fans eager to watch some of the best women footballers America and Europe had to offer.

But those heady days ended abruptly in her second season when she seriously damaged her knee while crossing a ball beyond San Jose CyberRays defender and World Cup bra-flashing pin-up Brandi Chastain. 'I went to cross the ball but my leg stayed and I turned and just heard the loudest pop and she kicked the ball out and everyone in the crowd heard it and it just went silent,' Smith says. 'I was just in bits, holding my knee.' Returning from that first major injury the following term after rigorous rehabilitation, Smith suffered another. Going in for a header, she collided with New York Power's Shannon Boxx and heard a crack. 'It was a torn meniscus, bone bruising and cartilage damage,' she says. It was also a second big injury within a year and Smith was, once again, living in a country she had grown to love but living a life bereft of the game she had always loved:

> I stayed out there but it was torture, still being a part of it, seeing it every day. You don't know whether not to be around it because then you isolate yourself and become depressed, or stay in it and feel depressed because you can't be playing. It's finding the balance and I really struggled with that. It was probably the darkest time of my life so far. I just felt I'd lost my purpose in life.

Counselling taught Smith to look for happiness away from football, which she did aided by friends from Philly and Seton Hall and her beloved boxer dog Bailey. At the same time, pep talks from Mark Krikorian, her coach at the Charge, and supportive emails from Hope Powell kept Smith believing she would eventually return to the game. It was not easy. 'There were many times when I thought about giving up,' she says. 'But then obviously when you start getting better and you can run again, you want to play and then start getting a bit of confidence and play again and then you think why did I have all those thoughts?'

Smith's first major injury saw her miss out on helping her England colleagues in their battle to reach the 2003 World Cup. The Lionesses did not manage to qualify after losing out to France in St Etienne, but when the threat of severe acute respiratory syndrome forced the tournament to move from China to America, Smith had a chance to feel part of the game again. Covering the finals as a roving reporter for the BBC after recovering from her second knee injury would see her interview the biggest names in the women's game for the folks back home. But the talking stopped for a moment as she watched the US team play a practice game ahead of the tournament – Smith was dumbstruck by news that the professional league had been disbanded. Smith recalls:

> I'm on the sidelines and Aaron, the press person for the US team, comes up to me, and he goes, 'Have you heard the news?' I said 'What news?' He said, 'That the league's folded'. I said, 'Shut up, why are you lying? It's before the World Cup, why have they announced that now?' But he was like, 'No I'm serious Kelly, it's been done, it's suspended'. Well, I just burst out crying and I was supposed to be interviewing Julie Foudy and Brandi Chastain and I'm in bits on the sideline. I'm trying to hide my tears from the people that are there watching the game and I had to interview these players after and try and hold it together.

Smith's fears over her career and her visa hit home first, but gradually she felt a sense of lost opportunity for the women's game:

> The attendances were good, I thought it was going in the right direction and it was like a slap in the face… And of any country that it's going to happen in, it'll happen there. So for it to be suspended like it was, it was like where is women's football going?

Where that league had gone was kaput, just as the only professional team and proposals to run a professional league had in England that same year. Fulham had made the step up in 2000 in response to the FA's announcement that a professional women's league would be in place by the 2003/04 season. The Cottagers were in the lowly South East Combination League then but they were soon flexing their daily-worked muscles and, with Norwegian Olympic gold medallist Margunn Haugenes and Olympic and World Cup winner Marianne Pettersen in the squad, they cruised to promotion to the Premier League's Southern Division. They were denied a double by amateurs Arsenal in a gripping FA Cup final that was billed as a victory for the underdog. Comments in the programme for that clash at Selhurst Park in May 2001 showed the governing body were keen to see a more level playing field, however, as FA chairman Geoff Thompson wrote:

> The Football Association, which has been running the women's game in this country since 1993, has ambitious plans for the game and has already made public its commitment to a professional league... The first year of research and consultation has been completed and the FA is confident of establishing the first professional women's league in Europe by 2003.

By 2002, Fulham had made it into the National Division having won the FA and League cups along the way. But they were still going it alone as professionals, with the likes of Arsenal, Charlton, Leeds and Doncaster Belles opting to turn semi-professional instead. 'In my heart of hearts I knew [professionalism] was the wrong way to go and I told [then Arsenal vice-chairman] David Dein we didn't need to go that route,' says Arsenal Ladies' manager Vic Akers. 'It is important that it doesn't just blow up.' That year, professionalism did just that. Writing in August 2002 on BBC.com, veteran women's football correspondent Tony Leighton reported, 'That target will not be met, with the FA now stating no more than: "What will be in place is the infrastructure for a professional women's league".' Fulham went on to sweep the board that season, winning all three domestic trophies, but they had already been put on notice that they were to be demoted to semi-professionals. Fulham chairman Mohamed Al Fayed said, 'The mediocre advances in women's football during this period have made it impossible.' By 2006 Fulham, who had finished a lowly third from bottom in the league, were dropped completely by the men and although an independent club was re-established at the eleventh hour, they were without a sponsor and scrabbling around for players for the new season. Kelly Smith bashed home a hat-trick in a 14-0 victory for Arsenal against a patched-up Cottagers two weeks into the season. It was a far cry from those heady professional days.

Smith, the only Englishwoman to have played professionally in America, was offered the chance to do so with Fulham but was too content with life stateside to accept. Few others would decline such a chance, especially today, even though fitting in work with football is not quite the nightmare it used to be. Postwoman Vicky Exley, the only top England player to have a job that does not involve sport, has never had any bother from her bosses. 'They're fantastic,' she says. 'They'll get the letter and say, "Oh you're away so and so, that's fine", they've never had a problem with that.' It was not always so simple in the 1980s. 'In those days it was a struggle for some of the players,' says Marieanne Spacey, star striker of that era. 'Some of the northern girls worked in factories and they only had two weeks off a year and that was when the factory closed down.' Unlike the players of yesteryear, however, players of today are fitting elite athlete training regimes in around their daily lives. Ex-Fulham pro Mary Phillip says:

> There's a lot of time and effort that you have to put into playing the game, You ask any male players at the level we are playing at would they do that without any funding and I don't think you'd get the same reaction that you get from us. A few players do have to take their holiday for the time they take for England so basically they're giving up any holiday time they have to play football.

Should they have to? It is an issue England and Charlton striker Eni Aluko and her brother Sone, a professional footballer with Birmingham City, often discuss. Sone Aluko has put his studies on hold to follow his dream of professionalism; Eni Aluko has missed England games to complete hers. She says:

> I'm very happy for him because he's worked just as hard as I have. But there are parts of my game that are better than his and even he says it, 'Why is it that women's football's not professional?' And the answer always is: it's not popular enough. Well when we had the Euros on and there was enough energy behind it, there were 30,000 people turning up to our games – more than they did for Blackburn men's games, so it can be popular if it's allowed to be popular. Men's football is popular because it's allowed to be, you can't miss it, it's there in your face – probably apart from Thursday and Friday, there's games on. I think you've got to look at it from an angle of what is it that's actually keeping the lid on women's football and once you see that then it will improve – but I really don't think it's the quality anymore, I don't think that can be used as an excuse anymore.

The success of the Euros in attracting large crowds when no other football was being played has given impetus to the idea that summer or midweek leagues could attract enough fans to generate income to run teams. 'The game now has to go on and experiment,' says Vic Akers. 'It's no good us playing when Arsenal [men] are playing Chelsea on a Sunday afternoon. We're going out expecting to gain supporters [but] all you're going to get is two or three men and a dog. You've got to play games not against the men's structure.' Charlton boss Keith Boanas says a different schedule to the now traditional August to April Sunday afternoon fixtures could work. 'It's finding a slot where we can nick some spectators if it's going to progress,' he says. Even the players are up for a change. 'I would love it to be a summer league so we are out of the men's shadow,' says Sue Smith. 'The crowds would improve because there's a lot of people who will just watch football.'

Over in America, where the eight-team WUSA professional league collapsed, men's football does not have the hold it has in England and match day attendances averaged between 6,000 and 8,000 per game. That fan base looked set to get their game back when, in 2007, it was announced that a new women's national professional soccer league

Back for England after double knee trouble, Kelly Smith (10) prepares to face Australia in Burnley.

was being organised for the following season. But in 2003, when the money ran out at WUSA and there were not enough sponsors to rescue it, Kelly Smith knew she had to work fast to get herself another team. Coming to Smith's rescue were New Jersey Wildcats.

By the time Smith ran out as skipper of the Wildcats in the W-League the following May, the striker had already made a tentative return for England. The national side were embarking on a string of friendly fixtures as preparation for Euro 2005, a tournament they did not need to qualify for having been chosen as hosts. Making her comeback with a first-half run-out against Australia's Matildas at Burnley's Turf Moor, Smith proved she had lost none of her vision or technique when she set up Rachel Yankey for the only goal of the game with a clever pass within seconds of kick-off. Smith got on the scoresheet herself four internationals later when she coolly slotted home a penalty against Denmark in a 2-0 victory at Portsmouth's Fratton Park.

But the progress of England's star player was cut short in a W-League game in July 2004. Smith broke her leg against Western Mass Lady Pioneers and her American adventure was at an end. She shrugged:

> I'm sitting around bored all day, all these things to think about, negativity and sadness and loneliness and I'm like, why am I here? So obviously, I got in contact with my family, said I was in a bad way and they said, 'Just

> come back home, come back here, get your head right, settled. If you want to go back, go back. If not, you've always got a home here.'

And so, after almost eight years across the pond, Smith returned to the family home near Watford that she and her younger brother Glen had plastered in posters of her Arsenal hero Ian Wright as teenagers. Football was in her system by then, the seeds sown in the days when her every spare moment was spent kicking a ball with Glen in the street. 'My dad always said I could kick a ball before I could really walk, so from a very young age, I adored it,' she says. Lea Farm Juniors were happy to have Smith in their school team as were local boys' clubs Garston and Herons. But some parents from opposition teams were not so accommodating and she was forced to give up after visiting sides refused to play with the precocious girl on the roster. '"Foul her"... "take her legs out"... this is not the boys playing, this is the parents of the other team,' she recalls. 'There was a lot of jealousy there. But every team that I played on, they wanted me on their team.' It was soul sapping for Smith and not exactly fun for her dad Bernard, a painter and decorator by trade, who was running his son's team at the time. 'It wasn't nice,' he says. 'Every child is entitled to play.'

His daughter had no intention of quitting completely, however, and found solace in Pinner Park girls' club, a team run by the late Norman Burns. 'It was a bunch of friends and their daughters that played,' she says. 'And Pinner was a good team back in the day. It no longer exists now but we had a lot of good level players.' They came up against them too, with future England winger Rachel Yankey playing for fierce neighbourhood rivals Mill Hill. Whenever the two sides went head-to-head, Yankey would whiz down one wing while fellow left-footer Smith careered down the other. 'There was always rivalry between the two teams,' recalls Yankey. 'And Kelly would always have it hard because every team would put about five players on her.'

Smith would still be the one to mark when she moved on to a women's side. A life-long Gooner, she dreamt of teaming up with Vic Akers' Arsenal Ladies. But Smith thought clubs had to chase you in those days not vice versa. 'I would have been there in a heartbeat but because I never got asked, I didn't go,' she says. Instead, the fourteen-year-old followed Pinner boss Norman Burns as the club merged with Wembley and he became no.2 to manager John Jones. Thrown straight into the reserves, Smith hit 38 goals in 27 matches, a tally that would see her break into the first team before the season was out. The following two terms saw Smith terrorise National Division defences with the kind of performances that prompted former Navy man Jones to shout out her talents from the rooftops. 'I have a girl here at Wembley, Kelly Smith, who is one of the most technically gifted players I have ever seen and the standard she has achieved given the limited training available is incredible,' he wrote in women's football magazine *On The Ball* in October 1996. He is of the same opinion today. 'We knew that she was gifted, she had tremendous balance and good feet,' he says. 'She demonstrates that now and she's on the female world stage in terms of football and she's played against some of the best players in the world and played with some of them.' But while Smith was Jones' dream player and was part of the team that tasted League Cup final victory over Donny Belles in 1996, she left in the middle of the following season to join her own dream team, Arsenal.

Ironically, by leaving Wembley midway through the season Smith missed out on the chance to reach her first FA Cup final. Wembley went on to feature in that showcase match later that season, beating Smith's Arsenal in the semi-finals before agonisingly losing 1-0 to Mary Phillip and Katie Chapman's Millwall at Upton Park. Wembley's former player consoled herself with the small matter of winning the League title for Arsenal instead – Smith's two goals against Liverpool, tucked past young keeper Rachel Brown, helped secure the title at Highbury. Smith no longer has the blades of grass she plucked from the hallowed turf as she wore the red and white of the men's club she had followed all her life. But she can happily recall the goals that were so impressive they made the tail end of a video compilation of the men's season:

American friends – Rachel Brown and Kelly Smith have both enjoyed soccer scholarships in the USA.

> Vic still talks about them – two of the best goals that he'd seen in a long while from a women's player. I picked up the ball from the halfway line and dribbled past a number of players and put it in the net and then the second one was a 40-yard volley. Kirsty Pealling played the ball over the top to me, it bounced and I just hit it. I just remember that so clearly.

It would be Smith's only title with the Gunners in that period. American universities had been competing to attract the youngster on a football scholarship after she was spotted playing for Pinner at Watford Leisure Centre while still a schoolgirl. Seton Hall University in New Jersey won the subsequent race for her signature and once she had finished her college course and debut Arsenal season, she headed out to Orange County. Losing Smith to America was disappointing for Vic Akers. It proved a heart-wrenching move for her mum, dad and brother too. Her dad Bernard recalls:

> When we dropped her off at Gatwick we said, don't look back, and we drove home and the three of us never said a word, from the moment that Kelly walked through that departure lounge, we didn't talk... It seemed that day that everyone we saw had a daughter and it was a real heart-string puller. But the opportunities at that point weren't over here for her, there seemed more opportunities out there.

Smith felt the same, even though it meant leaving her family and her team:

> Signing for a club that you supported from day dot is a big honour for me but I think deep down in my heart I wanted to move to America to play football... In England at that time it wasn't happening – we were only training Tuesday and Thursday nights and playing on Sundays and I felt I just wanted to act as a professional footballer and I could get that out in the US.

America's gain was not necessarily England's loss, however. Since giving the the then teenager a first cap, against Italy at Sunderland's Roker Park in 1995, Ted Copeland had seen Smith flourish on the international stage. The hotshot had scored four goals in her next five games, all European qualifiers. Not wanting to lose the player, Copeland ensured she was flown back from America whenever England met up and Hope Powell continued to send out the long-haul flight invites once she took over as boss. It was weary work for Smith but she loved playing for her country too much not to return. She says:

> I always used to watch the England women when they were on the TV. I remember watching the World Cup, the highlights on *Match of the Day* and Gill Coultard, the ball come over and she headed it in at the far post. I stayed up late watching that and I was like, I want to be playing for England. And then obviously getting called up, getting all the kit and feeling special and training and playing with all the good players, excellent.

Kelly Smith is happy to be back in an Arsenal kit after nearly eight years away.

Smith was called up just four and a half months after the squad returned from that World Cup in 1995. She got more than just her own kit the following year when, in a European qualifier in southern Italy, teammate Hope Powell took pity on the player for leaving her studs at home. 'I gave her my boots,' laughs Powell, who watched Smith go on to score. 'She didn't have studs so I gave her my boots. I thought, this kid has got flair, she needs a pair of boots.'

Returning home to England in winter 2004, Smith was soon tying the laces of her own shooting boots once she had recuperated from her broken leg at her parent's Hertfordshire home. Putting in a call to England room-mate, the Arsenal skipper Faye White, Smith asked if she could train with her old club. 'I asked would Vic be interested if I just come and train, not even looking to sign, just trying to get back into it, playing again and she said, "Yeah he'd love to have you",' Smith recalls. But the striker did not just return to the Gunners for night-time training sessions, she signed up to play for them week in, week out and offer her expertise to aspiring sixteen- to nineteen-year-olds as assistant director of Arsenal Ladies' academy in St Albans. Smith quickly gave her new charges a dash of inspiration – scoring her first goal for an English club in almost eight years on 23 January 2005, when she netted just before the break in an emphatic 7-0 victory over Bristol City.

It was a short-lived comeback. A nagging pain in her foot was diagnosed as a stress fracture and Smith had to put her return on hold. Akers kept his new acquisition running, though – even if it was in an automatic-geared courtesy car, the colour of which brought Smith more attention than she would have liked. 'Everybody made fun of me,' she grimaces, still cringing at the thought. 'Everyone knew I was coming, I was mortified. Nice of Vic obviously to get me a car – but one in orange!' Smith was mobile enough to ditch the car before the season was out and fit enough to don a Gunners jersey too. Coming on as a substitute at Charlton's home ground of Gravesend and Northfleet she influenced the match in the most dramatic fashion, unleashing a cheeky thirty-yard lob over the head of Charlton keeper Pauline Cope just seconds after entering the field of play. The goal clinched the title for Arsenal just as the precocious eighteen-year-old Smith's brace against Liverpool had done way back in 1997.

That foot injury hangover rumbled on into the Euros, but as England got into the swing of the World Cup 2007 qualifiers just a few months later, a fully fit Smith was finally letting her feet do the talking again on the international stage. Unusually, the player was waxing lyrical off it too. Throughout her career, Smith had always raised team spirits with her skills, an old trait that even her former Wembley manager, John Jones, can recall. 'She has an impact on the players around her, but unknowingly,' he says. 'She's not a braggart, she just loves the game of football and I think she's really passionate about it. Kelly doesn't talk a lot, she lets her football skills do the talking.' But England colleague Fara Williams had noticed a change in Smith since Euro 2005. 'You wouldn't get her speaking in a meeting in front of anybody and for her experience and ability you would think she would,' says Williams. The midfielder, who counts herself as one of Smith's biggest fans, says her reticence to speak up has now gone. 'She is a massive player, not the most talkative person but since the Euros she has come out of her shell massively,' she adds. Truth be told, the usually shy and retiring Smith's impetus to take the floor is down to a gentle nudge from Powell. Smith says:

> It's more of a responsibility that I have because now I'm one of the senior players and Hope has asked more of me. Although I don't really believe it, she says people will listen to anything I've got to say because I don't say a lot, so when I do speak they will listen. I'm quite a shy, reserved person, keep myself to myself, but if I can do that and feel I'm comfortable with it, to help the team, then I will, even if it does make me shake inside or sit there with sweaty palms which sometimes I do in team meetings because I think, am I saying something that's wrong? But at the end of the day, if you've got something to say, say it.

Sweating palms and a pounding heart may still haunt Smith the public speaker, but they are never a problem for Smith the player. And as the second of those World Cup qualification games kicked off at 1.30p.m. on 27 October 2005 – two days before her twenty-seventh birthday – Smith was on top form. Her one goal and one assist against Austria the previous month would seem paltry come the end of this match at the municipal stadium in Tapolca. By 1.33p.m. that sunny afternoon, Smith had already put England ahead.

Running into the box with defenders trailing in her wake, Smith shoots straight at Melinda Szvorda who blocks the shot only for the striker to pounce on the loose ball and nudge it past the now prostrate keeper on the second attempt. This is a game England are having to play without skipper Faye White, who picked up a knee knock in Arsenal's UEFA Cup quarter-final against World Cup winner Birgit Prinz and her Frankfurt colleagues. But the imposing Lindsay Johnson stands in for White while Mary Phillip takes the armband to lead from the back. Within five minutes of kick-off it looks as though the pair of them are about to have an easy day at the office. Defender Casey Stoney sets number two on its way, feeding lighting-fast striker Eni Aluko who puts the ball across the face of goal for Smith to side-foot home. Except the ball does not fly into the back of the net – the keeper's foot has blocked its path and it takes Rachel Yankey to prod the bobbling ball in. Livewire Aluko deservedly adds a third from close range from a whipped Alex Scott cross. Within another four minutes, Rachel Unitt has sent Smith on her way with a neat pass from the right. Smith knocks in a teasing cross which Aluko volleys at Szvorda, who does well to parry but only as far as stand-in midfielder Scott who drills home. Stalwart Katie Chapman makes it five on the half-hour, advancing forward to control a curling Unitt pass on the edge of the box before slamming a bouncing ball high into the goal. It is not even half-time but there is more to come, Scott bagging number six after a clever Yankey pass left her with only the keeper to beat and Smith making it 7-0 at half-time with a blistering shot from close range. Bench-bound Sue Smith plus the supporters sitting in the uncovered stand and lounging on the grassy banks that surround the pitch are witnessing a whitewash. But England are still not finished. 'We've been told that we have to have the killer instinct,' says keeper Rachel Brown.

Storming out again in the second half, England show they have that alright. Aluko and Stoney again combine to create an opening and the diminutive striker prods home her club captain's cross. Fara Williams is after a piece of the action by now and nods in a header for number nine. Jo Potter, on for Yankey, temporarily takes over Williams' penalty duties to score from the spot after a Hungary handball in the box. England's best goalscoring record of 10-0 is equalled. But there are three more to come, as Jody Handley, Smith and Williams wrap up a whacking 13-0 victory. It is a new England record but Kelly Smith is not about to get carried away. 'We could look at Hungary and think, yeah they're not the best technically,' says the hat-trick heroine. 'But it's not about them, it's about us and what we do and getting a performance and getting three points, because that's all it is, qualification points racked up on the board.'

Ooh's That Girl?

Goal-fests of the kind netted in Hungary were never going to be the order of the day when England travelled out to meet their next opponents, Holland, three weeks later. Having pulled off a shock win over France, the Dutch were flying high and Hope Powell's side could not afford to slip up on their trip to Zwolle, a bustling market town in the north of the country. The side they were set to meet there on a damp and chilly November night was managed by Powell's old friend, the former Holland international Vera Pauw. The ex-midfielder, who was capped 87 times by her country, had returned home after a handful of years as head coach of England's auld enemy, Scotland. But she was now in charge of her own national side and with both teams level pegging on points, this was the chance for either side to seize the advantage.

Having returned home from their last match in Holland victorious, it was England who had the psychological upper hand, however. The goal that settled that close-fought 1-0 win in Tuitjenhorn in September 2004 came from a somewhat unlikely source – England defender Rachel Unitt. It was the left-back's first goal for her country since debuting against France in 2000 and therefore a landmark for the Walsall-based player. Yet this visit to the Netherlands just over a year later was set to bolster the football-mad player's CV even more: it would be Unitt's fiftieth cap. She was only twenty-three but still brought experience to a young and developing England set-up. Not only that, she brought a poster-girl image to a game that was historically viewed by Joe Public as being played by women who were about as sporty as Nora Batty but not as good looking. Former England midfielder and manager Hope Powell acknowledges a greater acceptance of women's football since the days when she first laced up her boots. 'Now it's the norm and not taboo,' says Powell. 'When I was playing it was, "Ooh, what's that all about?"'

Today the 'ooh' factor is more a recognition from football fans that women can actually play the game and have personalities worthy of their interest. An impressive total of 70,000 spectators attended England's three Euro 2005 games and in the run-up to the competition, an average of just under 6,000 turned out to watch Powell's players in friendlies. Powell herself says:

> Less people are seeing it as just a male sport... That's to do with the exposure and Euro 2005 moved it on miles. I had a lot of comments afterwards, even though we didn't get out of the group, with people saying it was much better than watching the men's and that's a massive thing.

The public may be cottoning on to the idea that women's football can be as entertaining as men's, but the game is still unfavourably compared by the printed press. For a time, it looked promising. A May 1997 edition of women's football magazine *On The Ball* detailed how that year's England international against Germany at Deepdale, in which Sue Smith made her debut, received the greatest coverage since the run-up to the Women's World Cup 1995. The *Daily Telegraph*, *Independent*, *Guardian*, *Times*, *Sunday Express*, *Daily Star* and a raft of television and radio stations covered the match. In 2006/07, only the *Guardian* and *Sunday Mirror* ran a weekly women's football column, reflecting the Women's Sports Foundation's research that says female sport in general receives a mere five per cent of all sports coverage in the national papers. Journalists deny there is any bias. Speaking at a WSF conference at the Oval cricket ground in 2003, *Daily Telegraph* columnist Sue Mott said there is simply not the 'interest' in reports on women's sports events. 'We did a small box on the Women's World Cup final and did not get one single letter of complaint,' she told an

The fans gather in their thousands for all the fun of England's Euro 2005 matches.

audience which included England skipper Faye White. But the WSF, an independent body founded in 1984 to improve female access to sports, insists the Euros showed there is a 'national appetite for media coverage of women's football'. In a memorandum to the House of Commons Select Committee that met in 2006 to discuss women's football, the WSF said television audiences running into their millions plus coverage of the Euros by every English daily paper at least once during the competition 'really did prove that it is a myth to assume there is no interest in or desire to watch women's football'. But they also sounded a note of caution for the future and added, 'There is still a very long way to go before the entrenched culture of sports journalism accepts women's football and gives it the consistent coverage and support that it needs in order to flourish.'

Record-breaking victories help. The 13-0 trouncing of Hungary the previous month had attracted the attention of six national papers, even if the sum total of those reports amounted to fewer than 750 words – the kind of media coverage routinely given to shopping trips by England men's 'Wives and Girlfriends' during the World Cup 2006. It was back to business as usual for England after the Holland game, however, with reports carried in just the *Daily Telegraph* and *Evening Standard*. Dutch journalists' pre-match interest was overshadowed by their men's victory over Slovenia in the play-off for the Under-21 European Championship. But they did cover the game and the following morning a single national paper's report was longer than the entire coverage in the English printed press. Despite that, visiting manager Powell, somewhat bizarrely described in Dutch paper *Algemeen Dagblad* the day after the game as 'een dubbelgangster van Whoopy Goldberg' or Whoopy Goldberg lookalike, was buoyed by the attention her team were garnering from radio, television and sponsors since the Euros.

Having filmed the players during the Algarve Cup in Portugal, the BBC went on to promote its coverage of Euro 2005 ahead of kick-off by putting England players on television in the months that preceded the competition. Skipper Faye White showed off her knowledge of the men's game with former Manchester United defender Gary Pallister and pundit Mark Lawrenson on weekend preview show *Football Focus*. Hope Powell offered up her minute-by-minute analysis of men's Premiership matches to a distinguished panel featuring former professionals Peter Reid and Mark Bright on BBC1's *Final Score*. Alex Scott, Rachel Yankey, Kelly Smith and Rachel Brown could be found in less salubrious but equally rewarding surroundings, rifling through nick-nacks in search of hidden gems in *Bargain Hunt* (Smith and Brown edged it with a mighty £28 profit). It was the kind of exposure last seen on terrestrial television in the late 1980s when the WFA-run women's game was on our screens for an hour every week on Channel 4. Audiences peaked at 2.8 million before the plug was pulled in 1992 and satellite broadcasters Eurosport and Sky have carried the torch since.

Once the Euros were up and running, they were covered live on British Eurosport with commentary from *Fair Game* women's football magazine editor Jen O'Neill, by Radio Five Live and their enthusiastic reporter Jacqui Oatley, and by BBC television. Indeed, the corporation covered the women's game in more depth than ever before during that fortnight and were rewarded as a combined television audience of 8.2 million tuned in to England's games. The Women's Sports Foundation found it encouraging and told the Select Committee, 'The BBC coverage brought women's football into homes and workplace discussions like never before and along with the work of the FA, the marketing of the team and players meant that names like Karen Carney and Rachel Yankey became topics of everyday conversation.'

It was not only the broadcasters who introduced the England players into daily chit-chat, however. Images of Unitt, Yankey, Alex Scott, Katie Chapman and Fara Williams were plastered on promotional postcards, posters and even cash machines that summer. Unitt found the more off-the-wall promotions a tad unsettling. 'Mary Phillip came up to me one time saying, "I was at the bank the other day getting money out and your face appeared on the cash machine" which is pretty mad,' says Unitt. 'I think I would have ran off before I'd got the money out.' It did not end there. Defender Alex Scott arrived back from the Euros to find neighbourhood children knocking on her front door asking for autographs, manager Hope Powell was cornered in supermarkets by admiring old ladies and midfielder Kelly Smith was recognised in the street. It was a spell in the limelight that Smith feels the team have the right to bask in still. 'We feel like we deserve recognition,' she says. 'We are good enough to be household names, it's about us being known as women footballers and being respected for it.' England manager Hope Powell certainly appreciated the value of such promotion. 'Any exposure that puts us out there and gets people talking about women's football is more often than not a positive thing,' says Powell. The manager should know, she played in the England team who finished as silver medallists to Sweden in the European Championship 1984, but whose achievements were barely noted. Recalling the return leg of the final at Luton's Kenilworth Road ground, then England manager Martin

Reagan says: 'There were about thirty [media] correspondents there and I think twenty-nine of them were Swedish. I could not believe it, there was so little interest from our side.' Victories in the mini World Cup in Italy in 1985 and 1988 still only just scratched the surface of public consciousness back home. Marieanne Spacey, Powell's colleague during England's most successful period, and scorer of both goals in the 1988 final against hosts Italy, recalls an underwhelming reaction to their Mundialito successes:

> You did feel you were playing in the mini World Cup because the crowds were good and you were playing world class players. When we won it we were in dreamland [but] we were the ones banging on about it. I think we got on to a couple of 'Well done girls' patronising television programmes but then it was really just the Women's Football Association and one person running women's football in this country.

In 1988, England did achieve recognition in the form of a gong from the *Sunday Times* for their Mundialito triumph. The WFA's first ever secretary, Linda Whitehead, was honoured for her administration skills and the squad won Sports Team of the Year.

Acknowledgement of England's Euro 2005 performances came in the form of a visit to the Houses of Parliament to meet MPs such as Education Secretary Ruth Kelly. But despite finishing bottom of the group, the public took the team to their hearts, especially poster girl Unitt, whose physical attributes were immortalised in verse by poet Paul Collins in his ditty, 'Rachel Unitt Comes from Walsall' featuring the classic line: 'she's the best looking player that this country has ever seen'. She is one of the most popular too if the few thousand new internet friends, who include Radio One DJ Chris Moyles, are anything to go by. 'The amount of messages you get and things on MySpace is crazy,' she says. 'I think I've nearly got 11,000 friends now.' But Unitt's fame has spread beyond cyberspace. A love of clothes and chick flicks often sees the tough-tackling left-back nip from the family home to Birmingham's nearby Bull Ring shopping centre.

Up close and personal with fans' favourite Rachel Unitt.

Before the Euros, Unitt could manage it in relative anonymity. After the tournament, she was recognised even without her England kit on. 'I've been into town a few times and you get little kids shouting, "Are you Rachel?"' she grins. 'It's nice but it just makes me laugh. I appreciate it though.'

It is a modest enough response from a footballer who has her eye on a job as a firewoman once her playing days are over while seemingly knowing her worth enough to have secured an agent in the meantime. 'Work-wise, I'm going to join the fire brigade,' she insists. 'I couldn't get a job where you're just sitting in an office at a computer all day, I have to be active and on the move.' For now, though, football is all that preoccupies Unitt, to the extent that she trains full-time rather than fit her daily England routine around a job. As for her down time, whether it is titbits on the news, men's Premiership or League Two football or top-flight women's matches, Unitt is an obsessive observer of the game. 'Football, training, training, training, football, my life revolves around football,' she says. 'If someone called me and said "Do you want to come out this afternoon or this time next week?" the first thing I'd think about is what training I've got to do, which is sad.' It does not give her parents Debbie and Terry much to be glum about. Unitt's dad, a carpenter and ex-amateur who has coached Wolves Women and managed Aston Villa Ladies in his time, is almost as obsessed with the game as the second of his four daughters. 'My family are football mad, my dad's always played, my mum's always watched,' says Unitt, who still lives in the family home in the street she grew up in. Having only daughters, Terry Unitt had feared his chances of rearing a footballer were slim – until he saw his three-year-old on the ball. 'I thought it was never going to happen, but when I saw her kick a ball with her left foot I knew different,' says Terry, whose encouragement Unitt readily acknowledges. 'He's probably been the main influence for me,' she says. 'Right from a young age he took me to games, took me training there and back and he's always been there when I've needed him.'

Unitt first relied on her dad to give her a game when she was learning to walk. 'My mum and dad say my first word was ball,' she laughs. 'I used to follow the ball on the telly when I was a youngster.' But Unitt would not be content with armchair viewing and when she was old enough, she went calling for her own team. 'There's quite a few lads live in this street and I used to be a bit of a tomboy, so I used to play a lot with the lads,' she says. More organised games followed when Unitt went to primary school, as did a rather special call-up – for Walsall Schoolboys. The slightly-built, blonde-haired youngster with a floppy fringe and ponytail was ten when she ran out for the district side as a central midfielder. 'Think I come on and scored in that game,' Unitt says, recalling a fairly positive reaction from the watching parents and team. 'At first they probably saw me and thought, "Aah, it's only a girl", but I think when they saw me play their attitudes probably changed.' Dad Terry remembers the moment well. 'Some of the parents were a little bit negative saying, "What's she playing for?" but she scored a goal and people started to relax.'

By the time Unitt had made it into the cream of Walsall's boys' team, she was also finding her feet in her first all-girl side, Birchills Ramblers. The popularity of football among girls in 2007 has seen the creation of more than 7,045 girls' teams as opposed to eighty in 1993. That rise means most clubs get to play a decent variety of teams when they join a league. But in her day, Unitt remembers Ramblers having just two opponents, so the league ran with a familiarity that amuses her in retrospect. 'We had to play each other three or four times, which was crazy,' she laughs. There was no shortage of opponents when Unitt moved to Wolves Women at the age of thirteen. In those early years, the left-footer bossed the midfield rather than the left side of defence. It was an achievement given that she barely seemed to grow for about four years. 'She was very little and the other girls must have been about eight or nine inches taller than her,' recalls her dad. 'That always worried me.' But his daughter had a growth spurt at fourteen and Terry Unitt stopped worrying, knowing he had a winner on his hands. 'I said to my wife that if she shot up she would have a chance to play at some higher level,' he recalls. That Unitt did, passing her first England trial aged just sixteen.

Three goals in 16 call-ups for the England Under-18s, who were also managed by senior-team boss Powell, was not a bad return from midfield in two years. But an ambitious Unitt realised she would not be content with only Under-18 caps to show for her efforts and switched from the Northern Division of the Premier League to Everton in the National Division, one tier above. She commented:

> I just thought I needed to move to improve so I took that step of playing in the top division... Playing with better players, against better players, you know, you learn a lot more. The difference between the two leagues is pretty big and I don't think I could get away with playing in the Northern or Southern Premiership and playing for England. You need to play in the top league.

Rachel Unitt has been an integral part of the senior team since she was eighteen.

Despite her absence from the top flight, Unitt had clearly not escaped Powell's attention: a first senior call-up arrived two weeks before her first season with Everton had even kicked off.

It could not have been for a more daunting or thrilling game – France were to host England in a warm-up for their men's clash against a glittering FIFA World Stars team. 'I was away with the Under-18s and my mum called and said I had got a letter and that the game was against France at the Velodrome,' she recalls. And so in August 2000, the teenager's first taste of life among the seniors was alongside fellow debutante and Under-18 player Casey Stoney in a Marseille stadium packed with thousands of raucous fans. 'By the time the game had finished I think there was sixty-odd thousand there because they'd all come to watch the guys,' Unitt recalls. Her fellow defender Stoney, then an Arsenal player, found it just as surreal when she came on with thirty-five minutes left on the clock. 'I remember defending a corner and sat behind the goal was Frank Leboeuf and Marcel Desailly and I turned around and thought, is this really happening?' Stoney laughs. England lost 1-0 but both players had shown enough composure to remain in contention for a full senior cap. That honour arrived on Unitt's lap just three months later when she was called in for the suspended Julie Fletcher against Ukraine at Leyton Orient. A record crowd of 7,102 turned out at Brisbane Road for that fixture. This time, it was not the size of the crowd that would prove daunting but the importance of the tie. England were ninety minutes away from qualification for Euro 2001 and victory over Ukraine would see them through. Sue Smith and Rachel Yankey duly delivered, their goals landing a place in a Euro 'group of death' featuring Sweden and Germany. Those teams would prove beyond England's capabilities that summer, but Unitt's place in the starting XI during the tournament confirmed her own prowess. Within a couple of months she would face an offer she could not refuse – professionalism with Fulham. It meant upping sticks away from her parents and three sisters but Unitt felt she had little option. 'If you ask any woman footballer what they would have done, they would have gone,' she says.

Arriving at her digs in London, Unitt found herself in the less exalted surroundings of the Premier League's Southern Division. Fulham did not stay there for long, though, and were swiftly elevated to the National Division after a second unbeaten season. Playing professionally with Fulham where she trained day in, day out alongside mum-of-two Mary Phillip, England colleague Rachel Yankey and firm friend Katie Chapman, Unitt lifted the FA and League cups in 2002 and bagged the treble of FA and League cups and Premier League championship the following year, temporarily stymieing Arsenal's domination. 'She was playing every day and you could see the difference in her touch and the way she played,' says Terry Unitt.

But while professionalism was hailed as a success by the players and their families, it was not taken up by their less well-off opponents or the FA and Fulham pulled the plug in Unitt's second year.

And so, Fulham ran out in the 2003/04 season as a semi-professional outfit player-managed by former England star Marieanne Spacey. The striker had left the Gunners the year before to follow her own dream of playing professionally and was put in charge when manager Gaute Haugenes and the club's other star Scandinavian imports, including his wife Margunn, departed. That season, the club dropped out of the UEFA Cup at the quarter-final stage after a hefty 7-2 aggregate defeat by eventual finalists Frankfurt. They also lost the chance to defend their FA Cup crown when they were knocked out in the fifth round by Charlton and the Addicks added insult to injury by beating them 1-0 in the League Cup final. Even more dispiriting, Fulham had their League title whisked away by their other London rivals Arsenal in a thrilling last game of the season at Highbury that was so tight it could have seen the Gunners, Addicks or the Cottagers come out on top.

Despite the empty trophy cabinet, Unitt did manage to take one gong home with her in 2004 as her England performances secured the admiration of women's football experts who voted her International Player of the Year. It was an award Unitt would take north, however, after deciding that summer to re-sign for Everton who were being managed by former England captain Mo Marley. It was good preparation for the Euros, with the Merseyside club finishing third in the league and powering past Arsenal to reach the FA Cup final at Upton Park, where they lost 1-0 to Charlton. For Unitt, it was a lesson in mental toughness that would be supplemented by a tutorial in physical robustness just days later. With an eye on the Euros, England manager Powell reckoned Unitt needed toughening up and kept her behind to practise 50/50 challenges ahead of a friendly with Norway. 'Rachel is such a gentle soul on the pitch,' Powell says. 'She doesn't want to hurt anybody and she was a little bit too nice.' Almost three weeks after her tough-nut session, Unitt was not so nice to the visiting Czech Republic. Spurred on by a rousing

Jody Handley shares a joke with Rachel Unitt during a Eurp 2005 warm-up session.

home crowd at Walsall FC's Bescot Stadium, she trebled her senior goal tally with a brace either side of an audacious forty-yard looping shot by Kelly Smith in a 4-1 victory rounded off by a goal from fellow Brummy Eni Aluko.

England were unable to replicate such dominance in the Euros that followed, but their left-back did get her hands on a championship trophy in 2005. Rather than take a break after the tournament, a disappointed Unitt teamed up with an equally despondent Rachel Yankey and headed to the USA to play for Kelly Smith's former team, the New Jersey Wildcats. Unitt talked the decision over with old friend Katie Chapman and her partner Mark while she holidayed with the couple and their son Harvey in Mallorca and soon she was heading for America. The Wildcats offered Unitt her first taste of playing for an overseas side and she took to it with relish, lifting the W-League trophy after scoring alongside Kacey White and Heather O'Reilly against Ottawa Fury in a title decider attended by a capacity crowd of 2,233. It was a world away from England for Unitt and her housemate Yankey, who survived an exhausting night shooing a bat out of the winger's attic bedroom in New Jersey and a spot of overindulgence at the neighbourhood ice-cream parlour. 'Me and Yanks used to have these big waffles with ice-cream, two toppings,' she laughs. 'We still think about it, those waffles!' Playing among some of America's brightest young players was an experience of a different kind. 'Technically I think us English are better than the Americans,' she says, 'but from a younger age they focus on speed, fitness and strength and the game does seem much quicker out there.' Having to keep up with the likes of US international stars O'Reilly, Cat Reddick and Christie Welsh seemed to take it out of Unitt, coming on the back of such a busy year. 'When I came back from America, I've never felt so horrible,' she says. 'I was tired and my mind just went off on one. It took three or four months for me to get back into it.'

Unitt felt her lethargy had let her down in the previous World Cup 2007 qualification match against Hungary, even though England kept a clean sheet and scored 13 goals. Luckily, for a player to whom the mental side of her game is as important as the physical, support was close at hand from the psychologist brought into the squad by Powell after the World Cup 2003 play-off defeats. Misia Gervis introduced Unitt to visualisation techniques to overcome doubts over her performance. 'To be honest, I've always had problems recovering from mistakes,' she says. 'But I spoke to the psychologist about it and she's told me what to do and now, when I'm playing, I just forget about it and get on with it basically.' Which is what Unitt did when she ran out in Zwolle that night against Holland, winning her fiftieth cap in the process.

Just under 2,500 fans turn out to cheer the teams on in Oosterenkstadion that November night. Sitting in their midst is FA director of football development Trevor Brooking and injured right-back Alex Scott, her leg in full plaster after a knee injury. Next to her is Arsenal boss Vic Akers and assistant Fred Donnelly who have driven their player all the way to the match from east London. The tense game of cat and mouse that unfolds proves somewhat uneasy viewing for the England contingent. But they are almost brought to their feet after just seven minutes when striker Eni Aluko breaches Holland's defence, only to scuff her shot wide of the post. The action swings quickly to the other end and this time it is the young Dutch crowd who are jumping in anticipation as dangerous winger Manon Melis races into England's half and unleashes a shot but, like Aluko, can only drag the effort past the far post. The visitors are struggling to create chances against Holland's determined defence but the home side are penned back too, Unitt keeping a watchful eye on the speedy Melis as the action centres in the middle of the park where England have Vicky Exley in for the injured Katie Chapman. Holland finally test Rachel Brown in the thirty-fourth minute after a corner by former Bristol Rovers midfielder Annemieke Griffioen flies out as far as defender Liesbeth Migchelsen, but the England keeper smothers her soft shot and the cheers of the home fans. Skipper Faye White's determination to stymie Holland's attacks sees her concede a thirty-eighth-minute foul on Nicole Delies. White's mistimed tackle prompts the referee to flourish a yellow card that will keep her out of the next game – the grudge match against group favourites France. But the captain, who missed the previous qualifier through injury, puts her disappointment to the back of her mind and urges the team on. Kelly Smith answers the call and curls a shot wide just before half-time and Unitt almost scores with a header from a well-hit Casey Stoney free-kick but veteran keeper Marleen Wissink is equal to it. Unitt is weary but coping. 'Their right-winger Manon Melis was rapid quick and that's one thing I fear in a player because I'm not the quickest in the world,' she says. 'But I was doing alright.'

England were doing okay too ten minutes after the restart. Marloes de Boer was the heroine for Holland against France after scoring the only goal, but the central defender offers England a lifeline in this match when she fells substitute Amanda Barr and the visitors are awarded a penalty. Having finished off the scoring in that 13-0 annihilation of Hungary in the previous game, Fara Williams steps up to the plate with the same figure in her sights – her thirteenth international goal. Unleashing the trigger seconds later, the penalty specialist has her lucky number in the bag. England are inspired and Wissink is soon performing acrobatics to ensure her goal is not breached again. But Brown cannot switch off for a moment as de Boer tests her with a firm header and Dionne Demarteau grazes the near post with a twenty-yard free-kick. It is a final flourish from Holland but when the whistle blows the victory is England's.

Gathering for dinner that night, Unitt's landmark half-century is marked with applause from the team as former West Ham player Brooking hands over a commemorative plaque. Powell, Unitt's coach from Under-18s to seniors, is happy for her player but knows the time for real celebration will come if her squad makes it to China. 'I don't think we did ourselves justice,' she says after the match. 'We can play better and we will have to if we want to qualify for the World Cup.'

Honours Even

As England emerged from 2005 and into the second stage of their assault on the World Cup qualifiers, they had been almost three months without a competitive game together. A winter training camp in the Spanish resort of La Manga in January 2006 had maintained the momentum, while Premier League, FA Cup and League Cup action at home had kept the England players on their toes. It was a good job. Their manager had lined up a winter warmer of friendlies in Cyprus that were enough to send a shiver down any footballer's spine. Stung by the defeat that knocked England out of the Euros, Hope Powell immediately challenged the victors, Sweden, to a rematch. Eight months later, it was game on, but not just for one match – England were all set for a double-header against the country that defeated them by a single goal in June 2005. Taking on the fifth-ranked side in the world would be a challenge, but it was one Powell felt her players were equal to. 'I truly believe we did well in the European Championship,' she mused. 'I think we competed with the best in the world and Sweden certainly are one of the best in the world and we competed, we didn't disgrace ourselves and that just proved to me how far we've come.'

Rachel Yankey knew how far England had come as she packed her bag for Cyprus at the family home she shares with her mum Jean and brother Simon in London. England's most capped player in the squad at that time has been a familiar face on the left wing since 2002 and her performances for her country in the lead-up to the Euros had seen her named International Player of the Year 2005. And as she boarded the plane that February to take part in England's preparations to reach another major women's tournament, Yankey was on the verge of her sixtieth cap. Fittingly, it was Yankey who had been among the brightest performers against the Swedes at Ewood Park the previous June. In fact, the mazy runs of the winger and her then Birmingham City colleague Karen Carney had set tongues wagging in all three Euro group matches. Reporting in the *Guardian* the day after that final game, their women's football correspondent Paula Cocozza wrote, '[Women's] football has entered the nation's living rooms and crept into its conversations. And the wider world has learned the names of Rachel Yankey, Kelly Smith and Karen Carney…'

That said, Yankey was no stranger to the public gaze. Her promotion of Umbro's England women's shirt had seen her stare down at Joe Public from sports shop windows for a good two years before the competition. 'One time, me, Rachel Yankey and one of the other Fulham girls were driving in Walsall and someone recognised Yankey,' says her old Cottagers teammate Rachel Unitt. 'Yankey's got one of them faces that you know.' Sponsorship of the Arsenal team put Yankey in the spotlight even earlier than 2003, though. A photo of a chubby-faced Yankey as a baby was used on a 'then and now' display when Nike opened its new superstore in London's bustling Oxford Street. 'I saw the front of it and thought, oh that's pretty cool and then turned it around and thought, oh mum what have you done to me?' she laughs. Mum had not had a hand in the Nike advert that ran in women's football magazine *On The Ball* in 1999. That featured a youthful and sporty nineteen-year-old Yankey standing in Arsenal FC's Highbury changing room staring covetously at a football. It was a sign of things to come, even if the blurb that accompanied the advert was not quite on the mark. That read, 'Playing football won't put me on telly and neither will helping my boyfriend with his homework. So I'll do both of these strictly out of love.' Within three years, football did put Yankey on the telly.

Teaming up with the England men, Kelly Smith (10, left) and Rachel Yankey (11, right) help launch a new Umbro women's kit.

The winger's Beckham-esque free-kick for Fulham in the 2002 FA Cup final against Doncaster Belles was watched by 2.5 million enthralled BBC viewers as it curled into the net. Television audiences also saw her pull a Player of the Match performance out of the bag for Fulham in the FA Cup final the following year as the Cottagers beat London rivals Charlton 3-0. And in 2005 came the Euros. Yet Yankey still scratches her head when asked to make sense of her status in the public eye:

> I don't know how many mixed-race black players there were playing. Having my hair done in plaits it was easy to recognise me over other people, playing up front is more attractive, so stuff like that always helps but I don't know, I don't really think about it, I'm just happy to do it and if it helps women's football and gets people knowing a bit more about it then it's good for me and other people.

As she headed out to face Sweden in February 2006, Yankey knew that football had made her more than a familiar face; she had become a role

No stranger to the media spotlight, Rachel Yankey talks to the BBC.

model too. On this trip, instead of it being plain old Rachel Yankey passing through passport control, it was now Rachel Yankey MBE.

Yankey was one of only four football faces recognised in the Queen's New Year's honours list in 2006 and, at that time, one of just seven females ever to receive the gong for services to the women's game. It took her a while to believe she had been included in that elite group, though. A mix-up had seen the letter offering her an MBE delivered to her old club Birmingham. But Yankey was back with Arsenal by then, so when it was forwarded to her in a bog-standard envelope, the player thought her teammates were pulling a fast one. Thrusting it at defender Alex Scott, Yankey demanded to know who was behind the joke. 'I was looking at the envelope and thinking, one of you lot's winding me up,' she says. 'I said to Alex, read that, is someone winding me up? And she's like, "Oh my god, that's wicked".' As it turned out, Yankey's colleagues were not involved, the offer was official and the player really did have a date to meet Prince Charles at Buckingham Palace with her proud mum Jean, brother Simon and boyfriend Ozzie at her side.

Yankey was chosen for the MBE for her contributions to the women's game, her work as a football coach as much cause for the nomination as her status as role model and the most capped player in action at that time. As a professional at Fulham, Yankey took the game to the community, her Euro 2001 player statistics noting her as coaching 'in the community to encourage more girls to take up the sport'. Today, as with many female footballers, including most of her international colleagues, England's no. 11 continues to bring the beautiful game to children through coaching sessions run in and out of school time. Her Rachel Yankey Football Programme offers primary school-aged youngsters in the London borough of Brent the odd surprise too. To give her players match practice, Yankey has pitted some against her England colleague Mary Phillip's young charges from Peckham Town. 'We made them a team, we got them a kit, so they all felt part of something,' says Yankey. While others have even been chauffeur-driven by their coach – to watch her take on the Danish elite in Arsenal's crunch UEFA Cup semi-final against Brøndby at Boreham Wood FC. Herding children off a bus you have just driven before heading for the changing rooms to prepare for one of the most important matches of your career is not the kind of behaviour you would come across in top-flight men's football. But this is the women's game and Yankey was happy to oblige even if she did have her worried manager Vic Akers on the phone wondering where his player was. She laughs:

> Vic was like, 'Where are you?' We're in the UEFA Cup semi-final and I'm driving a minibus full of kids to the ground. But when you see them back in school, telling their mates, it was like it didn't matter that it was women's football or men's football, it was just that they went to the game and felt proud. They knew some of the players on the pitch and it was something that was theirs.

Yankey first got a taste for coaching youngsters while just a kid herself. Signing up as a Youth Training Scheme worker at Arsenal FC

Rachel Yankey arrives in time to help Arsenal defeat Danish champions Brøndby in their UEFA Cup semi-final tie.

offered grounding in a profession that Yankey now hopes will see her through life once her playing days are over. It was a lesson she has never forgotten. 'The coaches down there were really good and looked after us and taught us how to actually carry out these sessions,' she says. 'I suppose in coaching terms I should be thanking them really because they brought me up in the right way.'

A bid to bring even more female coaches up the right way comes under the scope of the FA's Talent Development Plan, which includes a national coaches mentoring programme. By 2006, over sixty female coaches were registered on the scheme, four of them with elite UEFA 'A' licences and one – Hope Powell – with the top UEFA Pro Licence. Nationally, FA figures show that women are joining the coaching ladder, although in far fewer numbers than men. Between April 2006 and March 2007, 3,095 women gained their Level One coaching badge, accounting for twelve per cent of successful candidates. At the higher Level Two, women made up six per cent of the total and at Level Three, it was four per cent. Seasoned coach, UEFA 'B' licence holder and former England player Wendy

Owen reckons an increase in female coaches would be good for the game. 'I think that the girls need the role models,' she says. 'The more females you can get into schools and clubs so that they've got the role models to aspire to [then] it's not seen as something abnormal, it's seen as something for a woman to do. That's really important.' There are certainly plenty of girls out there to coach. When in 2001 the FA set up its 'Get Involved' marketing campaign to encourage more girls to play, their hotline number fielded around 6,000 calls. At that time, some 55,000 women and girls were on the FA's books, compared to around 10,000 when they took over the game in 1993. By 2002, football was officially noted by the FA as the number one female sport in the country and five years later there were almost 147,000 players. And whereas in 1993, there were eighty girls' teams, that figure had increased almost a hundredfold in 2007 to 7,045. In a bid to keep the numbers rising, the FA used funding from Sport England and the Football Foundation to set up forty-six full-time girls' development officers to bring the game to youngsters through its county associations. Getting youngsters to carry on lacing up their boots into adulthood is seen as a boon for the international set-up. 'The younger kids coming through at under-12s have been playing since birth and it's organised and it's fantastic,' says Hope Powell. 'We want them to keep playing and that's the most important thing. They play, but drop out and we want them to stay in the game. There's some real talent lower down and that's credit to the grassroots.'

Looking back to the days when she first took up the game as an eight-year-old, Yankey cannot remember being offered coaching sessions of the kind she now holds for children. 'I never went to a holiday camp or a Saturday school,' she says. 'I don't think my mum would ever have been able to pay for me to go and play football, it can get quite expensive so that's why we try to keep costs down and just let the kids play really.' When she was a kid, Yankey was happy to just play, kicking around near her north-west London home with her friends and older brother Simon in Queen's Park. Oblivious to the presence of nearby girls' teams, Yankey went on

Rachel Yankey puts a budding player through her paces at a coaching session.

to play five-a-side for a boys' team on the nearby South Kilburn Estate in the London borough of Camden. Being a tomboy, Yankey got away with playing in a boys' league because most of the teams assumed that striker 'Ray' was a lad. All that changed when she was recognised in a cup final and hauled off mid-match for being too old and a girl to boot. 'I'm not saying we would have won if I'd stayed on but we lost and I was gutted,' she says. The chance to sign up for north London club Mill Hill's girls' team softened the blow, with manager Russell Mountfield offering to give the speedy striker a game after the cup final was raised at a league committee meeting. It was an offer that shocked the youngster. 'I didn't know there were girls' teams,' admits Yankey. Mum Jean initially feared her daughter might not take to the idea. 'We thought she wouldn't want to go after playing with the boys but she did,' she says. 'She liked it and from then on it was plain sailing.' Basically, Yankey would go anywhere to carry on playing. 'I wasn't the world's best in school academically so it was an escape from that and something that gave me joy and something I was interested in,' she says. Yankey did not know it at the time but she was about to play against a potential world footballing best. Kelly Smith played five-a-side for nearby Pinner Park and the two future England stars would regularly come face to face on the pitch. 'It was a big rivalry,' Kelly Smith recalls. 'She was tiny back then. Both of us looked like little boys.'

Like Smith, Yankey relished the rivalry and loved to play, be it eleven-a-sides in the Greater London League with Mill Hill or friendlies for Hampstead School's boys or girls. 'I was best mates with the boys in the football team and we had grown up together,' she laughs. 'They still ring me up now and say, "Yeah, I taught you that move".' The school's five-a-side girls' team were less cocksure and preferred to pass to their star player and watch her fly. 'Everyone would give me the ball and say, "Go Rachel",' she says. 'I hated it, that's why when I'm in front of goal I always pass because it just felt so selfish.' But being given the chance to show off her footballing flair did Yankey no harm when Arsenal manager Vic Akers refereed a Gunners five-a-side schools league featuring Hampstead's fifteen-year-old star striker. 'I knew just by her touch of the football that she was always going to be a player,' recalls Akers, who checked out if Yankey needed a club to play for, only to be told, 'No, I play for Mill Hill.'

A season later, Yankey was ready to end her happy five-year association with Mill Hill and plumped for a move across north London. 'I was wondering what to do and I thought I may as well try out at Arsenal,' she shrugs. A few matches for the Gunners' reserves soon turned into substitute appearances for the first team and then a regular spot. Within a year, Yankey was spearheading Arsenal's attack alongside Marieanne Spacey and striving to fill the striker's England boots. It was a curious time given that while she was at Mill Hill, she could have walked past Spacey in the street and not known who she was. 'If you had asked the girls in our team they would have been able to tell you about Arsenal, but I was a bit oblivious to what was going on,' Yankey admits. 'I was just happy to be playing football, I didn't really know that there was a senior team and how good they were.' Yankey's

Rachel Yankey (front centre) played alongside Faye White (back row, third from right) and Casey Stoney (back row, second from right) in her first spell with Arsenal.

education was complete by 1997, however, when she burst on to the international scene alongside England regulars Hope Powell, Gill Coultard and fellow newcomers Sue Smith and Rachel Brown.

Yankey still has the shirt she wore on her England debut, a 4-0 friendly victory over Scotland at Livingston in August 1997 in which she scored alongside Sammy Britton and Kerry Davis, who hit a brace. Her mum Jean still has a tape of the game that pre-empted a successful England career too. But despite making it on to celluloid and the scoresheet, Yankey was shocked when she was called into the starting line-up for the following game, a crucial World Cup 1999 qualifier away to Germany. 'I started that game which I totally didn't expect,' she says. Alongside her on that trip to Dessau in eastern Germany, where England lost 3-0, was future room-mate Sue Smith.

These days, the two are seen as the life and soul of the team with their fondness for making up quizzes, dressing up and generally playing the fool. 'We're always playing pranks on each other,' says Rachel Unitt. 'But Yankey and Sue Smith, those two are like the characters in the team. They're always up to something, but you need people like that.' Back in the early days, though, the teenage rookies tended to shy away from the team's established faces, even if they roomed together. 'I shared a room with Kerry Davis but she was so much older than me, if she turned the channel over I wasn't going to turn it back,' laughs Yankey. 'Now with the England team, you can feel quite comfortable going in anyone's room and having a laugh with anyone, then it was more adults and children.' Yankey may have been too much in awe of the stalwarts to fiddle with the remote control in her room, but she always felt at ease with them on the pitch. 'We were just happy to be there and play,' she says. 'There wasn't any pressure on performance.'

The teenager may have been stunned to play away to Germany, but she was gutted to miss out on the return leg at Millwall the following March. That game was settled by the slimmest of margins this time – 1-0 to the Germans. It proved too great a loss and England missed out on the World Cup 1999 after finishing bottom of their group the previous August. The next major tournament in the international calendar would feature England, though, and their nippy striker played her part in getting them there. In November 2000, Yankey and Smith both scored to edge out Ukraine to rapturous applause from a then record crowd of 7,102 fans at Leyton Orient's Brisbane Road ground. Smith opened and Yankey added the second just seven minutes after coming on in place of Arsenal's Marieanne Spacey with nineteen minutes left on the clock. The crucial victory, which offered Rachel Unitt her full debut, saw England win 4-1 on aggregate to secure their passage to Euro 2001 out in Germany. When Yankey traded places with Spacey that night, though, they did not shake hands as Arsenal teammates. Four years with the Gunners had yielded the Yankey trophy cabinet six winners medals all by the tender age of twenty, but the Arsenal striker still felt the urge for fresh challenges.

She found one in the summer of 2000 when she landed in the French-speaking city of Montreal in Canada to play for Laval

Dynamites in the North American W-League only to find her mother tongue was nowhere to be heard. 'The coach did all the team talks in French and I was like, ah, I knew I should have paid attention in school,' Yankey laughs. 'But that was growing up and learning. When I was out there I was like, get me out of this place, but come away from it, when you're back, it was brilliant.' Life really would be brilliant when Yankey eventually returned from knocking in the goals and learning the French for 'man on' out in Canada. While she was across the pond, the twenty-year-old received a phone call that would see her return to London at the end of the season not to play for Vic Akers' Arsenal as expected, but to join their new London rivals Fulham.

'Pay me to play football, every day, what are you on about?' was Yankey's response when Fulham, England's first professional club, came calling that summer. But that was exactly what was on offer. Mohamed Al Fayed had taken on board the FA's plan for a professional league and the club wanted Yankey to sign up. Which the Londoner did, although she insists it was not a snap decision. Fulham may have been bankrolled by Al Fayed to become professional, but the club had to make their way through two divisions before they could even play at the same level as Yankey's old side Arsenal. 'The standard in the league was a big drop,' says Yankey. 'But it was a once-in-a-lifetime opportunity and if the league is not as good it balances out with training every day.' Telling Arsenal boss Vic Akers she would not be re-signing that season was, Yankey says, 'the hardest conversation I've ever had'. Akers took it on the chin. 'He was always honest and said, "I want you to come back, try it out and when it doesn't work out, come back",' she says. 'He knew there was nothing else for me, the YTS was good but I didn't have a job so it came at the ideal time.'

It did not take long for Fulham to catch up Arsenal and the rest of the National Division. By the time they won that League title along with the FA and League cups in 2002/03, the side was chock-full of internationals and Yankey had made the transition from striker to winger. 'We found because of her ability to drop her shoulder and go past players that she was effective at taking on players and with her crossing ability [to] pick out passes on the ground and in the air,' recalls former Fulham boss Frank McMorrow. Having changed position domestically, the professional player did the same internationally. In doing so, she had not just filled the boots of injured England winger Sue Smith; Yankey's rapid runs down the flanks saw her claim them as her own. 'When I first played it, it was very alien to me,' Yankey admits. 'Making long runs and having to defend, it was something I really hadn't done.' But Yankey adapted, as did her old England room-mate Smith whenever she found herself playing second fiddle to her friend. 'People always say, "How can you be best mates with Yankey?" but I always have been,' says Smith.

But while all was going well internationally, the domestic scene was less rosy back at Yankey's home club. Although Fulham took all three titles that season, they were demoted to semi-professionals after it became apparent that the FA's plans for a professional league would not materialise in 2003. Yankey stuck with the Cottagers as a semi-pro, but it would be her last season. 'It was too much of a change,' she says. 'You'd gone from being a professional to go back down and train twice a week. I said I have to go somewhere else and get the love back again.'

And so, by the end of 2003/04, Fulham were unable to retain their titles and many of their key players. Everton beckoned for Rachel Unitt and skipper Mary Phillip decamped to Arsenal. Meanwhile, Birmingham City had landed enough sponsorship to let manager Marcus Bignot pitch for the likes of Yankey. To the surprise of many, the Queens Park Rangers professional pulled the signing off. 'The obvious thing was go back to Arsenal,' Yankey recalls. 'But then Marcus rang and offered it to me. I thought he was joking.' The ambitious Bignot was deadly serious and told the winger he could improve her game if she made the move. 'We've always been renowned for producing players and making them better and we just felt we could make her better,' he says. With one eye on the forthcoming Euros, Yankey agreed:

> People said, 'Why are you going there? You're only going for the money,' but it wasn't really about that... Marcus was telling me about myself and how I played and that's what made me think this guy has done his research. He had gone through my strengths and weaknesses and I wanted to be a part of what he was doing and let him help me and make me better.

Bignot believed Yankey could make his team better too. 'With Yanks, it wasn't [just] a question of her abilities, it was how could she help others,' he adds. As it turned out, winding her way up to the Midlands twice a week with London-based teammates Alex Scott and Ellen Maggs was worth the effort. Yankey and Birmingham's other new recruits featured for the England team as they rehearsed for the Euros at the Algarve Cup while at home they secured a fourth place finish in the league, a quarter-final berth in the FA Cup and reached the semi-final stages of the League Cup. Yankey, who won International Player of the Year plaudits after being nominated by the England squad and staff that May, viewed it as ideal preparation for the Euros. 'I wanted that sort of challenge and found it enjoyable,' she says. 'There was so much laughter and good banter on the way to games. Everyone was joining in and I really liked that about that team.' There was little joy once Yankey and her club colleagues Scott, Amanda Barr, Karen Carney and Jo Fletcher had played in the Euros, however. Birmingham had lost their sponsorship and mooted backing from the men's club did not materialise. Without the £50,000 needed to run the team, the club folded and several key players signed up elsewhere. Just days later, Birmingham reversed their decision after a parent threw them the lifeline of a £10,000 donation and the FA granted the club three weeks' grace to get their affairs in order. But by then they had lost their star winger Yankey, who was away for the summer playing for the New Jersey Wildcats in America as the financial crisis unfolded. Yankey would be welcomed back with open arms at her old club Arsenal upon her return. But coming on the back of the disappointment Yankey already felt over the Euros, it was still a sorry end to a promising summer. Winning the prestigious W-League trophy with the team Kelly Smith once captained helped lift the gloom. 'I think that was a good thing for me when I went out to the Wildcats,' she says. 'I had to go straight back into playing football and obviously focus on that again.' Getting even with Sweden in February 2006 would help too, even if Yankey would only get one shot at it.

Around 400 spectators, including France coach Elisabeth Loisel, were at the GSZ Stadium in Larnaca to watch the two sides go head-to-head in that first friendly. Sweden were ranked a good seven places ahead of England in the world, but Powell's team had only lost two games in open play during the previous eighteen months, one of those to their opponents. So emerging from the opening match with a 0-0 draw under their belts was a boost for the England team, particularly with skipper and central defender Faye White absent with an ankle injury. A goal-less scoreline it may have been, but there were chances aplenty, with Yankey and Vicky Exley seeing efforts cleared off the line, right-back Casey Stoney watching her well-timed header hit the post and teenager Karen Carney heading over the bar. For the opposition, skipper Victoria Svensson poses her usual threat in the final third, but only really puts Rachel Brown to the test once and the lass from Burnley is equal to it. It was still a nail-biting contest. 'This was a good match with high tempo and many chances, it could have just as easily finished 2-2,' enthused Sweden coach and former Hammarby player Thomas Dennerby on the Swedish FA website afterwards.

Both sides show that their enthusiasm is undimmed when they meet again two days later, this time in Achna. Yankey is keen to play but patiently sits out the match while Powell gives a full ninety minutes to players such as Lindsay Johnson, Jo Potter and Anita Asante. But if it is tough for Yankey to have to watch from the sidelines, her teammates at least oblige with an exciting game for the spectators. Sweden are the first to make their mark, taking an early lead just as they had in that Euro 2005 game at Ewood Park the previous June.

Manchester United fan Svensson unlocks the England defence, setting up Maria Aronsson for the opener. A whitewash looks possible as nippy defender Anna Paulson, Nilla Fischer and Aronsson all come close to putting the ball beyond Brown. But England are not here to make up the numbers and Powell's side fight back. Their reward comes just after the hour as Katie Chapman forces a fumble from keeper Sofia Lundgren that lets in her old Fulham teammate Rachel Unitt for her fourth international goal and England's equaliser.

As the final whistle blows, it remains honours even but it is England who emerge with their heads held high. A losing streak to Sweden that dates back nearly twenty years has been well and truly halted. 'We grew together in those games against Sweden,' says Yankey, who is not alone in feeling that a change is in the air. 'In the Euros losing [to Sweden] we were disappointed, but we'd been beaten by the better team at the time,' says Fara Williams. 'With the friendly draws we were disappointed and thought we should have won them. That's the difference, in just a few months, going from losing 1-0 to then thinking we should have beaten them and being disappointed.' It was exactly the kind of attitude and progress Powell had been hoping for.

Taking the Stage

If Sweden taught England how far they had come as a group, their final friendly before resuming their World Cup qualification campaign would steepen their learning curve yet further. Iceland were ranked nineteenth, just seven places behind England, and enjoyed a reputation as a side that were difficult to break down. England usually managed it, emerging from their encounters unbeaten since they first met in 1992. So when Iceland visited Carrow Road on a wet and windy night in March, Powell's squad were determined to maintain that record. Aiming to be among those to pierce the Icelandic side's defensive core this time around was one of England's emerging stars from the Euros, Karen Carney.

The teenage winger had scored exactly a year ago to the day of Iceland's visit to Norwich, bagging a goal against Northern Ireland on a dusty pitch in Portugal at the Algarve Cup. It was a special goal that day, not just because it was the seventeeen-year-old's first full game for the senior side – it was also her mother Marie's birthday. 'She said to go and get a goal for her so I did,' said 'Kaz' after that 4-0 victory in the sunny Algarve. Her joy when she rang home to convey a somewhat unorthodox present to her mum that night was even greater than it would normally have been. That was because Marie Carney was undergoing treatment for breast cancer and Kaz was keen to bring cheer to the family in any way she could. So to score another birthday present in front of her mum, dad and sister Sarah exactly a year later would surely be too much to ask. Wouldn't it?

Maybe not, given the year Carney had enjoyed since playing her way into England's Euro squad at the Algarve. Just the previous month, in February 2005, the wiry winger had become the youngest player to be capped for the senior squad by Hope Powell in her seven years at the helm. The teen had seized the chance to impress a few months earlier when called up to a four-day training camp at Lilleshall after England's Arsenal contingent dropped out to go on UEFA Cup quarter-final duty in Sardinia. Powell promptly pencilled the winger in for a friendly against Italy at Milton Keynes and Carney showed the manager what she was about by coming off the bench to score the final goal in a 4-1 win. Rubbing shoulders with the seniors was a new experience for Carney, who admits that what knowledge she had of the team before then had come from watching television. 'I'd seen a couple of games on Sky Sports when I was quite young,' she says. 'But I didn't really know anything about them.' Less than three weeks after Italy, Carney gained a better insight when she joined the thirty-woman England squad leaving for Portugal and the annual twelve-nation Algarve Cup. Looking on in astonishment as she ate her breakfast in the same room as US captain Kristine Lilly and Sweden's Hanna Ljungberg, Carney said she found it 'amazing' to be among players she had watched in World Cup action on DVD just a few weeks earlier. Carney would not be awestruck once she was out on the pitch, however, and she soon set about taking apart the sides in England's group.

The winger had an immediate impact in the opener, side-footing into the far corner against a dogged Northern Ireland defence in a game England would eventually win 4-0. Carney then set up her Birmingham City colleagues Amanda Barr and Rachel Yankey in England's second 4-0 win of the week, this time over hosts Portugal. Two further run-outs on England's return in friendlies against Scotland and Norway and Powell had seen enough – Carney had played her way into the manager's Euro 2005 squad ahead of established faces such as Sue Smith. In Powell's eyes, picking relative newcomers such as Carney and Eniola Aluko was no gamble. 'It's

Karen Carney skips past Mariann Knudsen and Danish captain Katrine Pedersen on her way to Euro 2005 stardom.

not an age thing,' she says. 'They were playing well enough and had experienced that kind of tournament play. They don't go into games with preconceived ideas about Germany etc, they just want to play and that's why they have done well.'

And they did. Carney and Aluko threw off the shackles of fear when they faced Finland, Denmark and Sweden and made their mark as the most thrilling players on the pitch during the Euros. It was not easy. Forthcoming A-level exams meant both had their heads in books throughout the tournament and Carney still had the health of her mum at the back of her mind. But Marie Carney did her best to relieve those worries, telling her daughter, 'Promise me one thing, don't worry about me and just go out and do your best, that's all I ask.' Carney honoured her mum's request in fine style, her ninetieth-minute winner against Finland in England's opening Euro 2005 match at the City of Manchester Stadium on 5 June elevating her to star status across the nation in the process.

'Carney in a class of her own' declared the *Guardian*. 'In the popular imagination, with 2.6 million watching the match live on BBC2... Karen Carney became the Wayne Rooney of women's football,' enthused their reporter Paula Cocozza. Carney, who went into the competition with FA Young Player of the Year plaudits still ringing in her ears, looks back on the experience as a turning point. 'Nobody really knew who I was or what I was about,' she says. 'Then I went in the Euros and came out a footballer. It was kind of weird.' Sadly, even a footballer with enough skill to be labelled a female Wazza could not inspire England to progress out of their group in the Euros. But regardless of that disappointment, when Carney's family sat in the stands at Norwich FC that wet evening in March 2006 to watch England face Iceland, they knew how far she had come.

By the time she was sixteen, Carney had given up a life-long love of dancing and uprooted herself from the close-knit family home in the Birmingham suburb of Hall Green to sign up for a live-in course for elite footballers in Leicestershire. The youngster had secured one of twenty scholarships worth an estimated £15,000 to £20,000 to attend the FA's National Player Development Centre at Loughborough University. Those talented enough to be selected for the NPDC live on site and get to play football while studying, an idea that emerged from Powell's unhappiness at seeing American universities and colleges make off with England's most promising female players. 'We were losing a lot of our most talented to the States on a scholarship,' she says. 'So we decided to do the same at Loughborough.'

Having checked out France's set-up at the world-famous Clairefontaine academy and sussed out what other countries do to nurture their up-and-coming stars, Powell and her colleagues came up with the NPDC. There, players train before and after classes and eat in a special athletes' cafe while having access to top-notch coaches, doctors, physiotherapists and facilities. Because they are still developing physically, Loughborough students are only released to their clubs on match days and get three passes a term to join up with

Above and below: Loughborough is a home from home for Karen Carney (above) and offers all the extras that elite athletes like her and fellow England player Jo Potter (below) need to succeed.

their teammates midweek. It is a situation the England set-up deems as being good for the players. Centre manager Lois Fidler says:

> We are trying to educate them about rest and recovery, to make sure that they are doing the volume of training that's required at international level but also having a relationship with their clubs... It's not perfect, it will be reviewed and hopefully the clubs will have some say in how it works for them, how we can improve it and how we can work on it to take it forward.

Carney, who signed up to sit her A-levels and a sports science foundation degree, admits her dad Michael was not totally sure about his daughter joining such a regimented system at such a young age. 'My dad initially thought it was a bit too early for me but my mum was all for it and now they are both really glad that I'm here and know that I probably wouldn't be where I am today without it,' she says at an open day during which she speaks to TheFA.com, Radio Five reporter Jacqui Oatley and *Fair Game* magazine while showing prospective pupils around her student bedroom. Standing in the doorway of Carney's cosy home from home is Everton's Jill Scott. Gangly and gregarious Scott was captain of the Under-19s and on the fringe of the England team during the World Cup 2007 qualifying months. And like Carney and the other scholars at Loughborough, who included emerging senior prospect Jo Potter, she epitomised the progression of the England set-up since the FA threw itself into girls' football development in 1997.

'In our day we were deprived of the expertise, knowledge and support and youth development which they have now,' says England Under-19 and Everton boss Mo Marley, who coaches part-time at Loughborough. The former England captain, who was awarded an MBE in 2005 for her services to women's and girls' football, won the first of her 41 caps against Italy in 1995 alongside Kelly Smith. That was just three years after what former England international Sue Lopez describes in her book *Women on the Ball* as the folding

Loughborough student Jill Scott (white shirt) came up through the ranks of England and Sunderland before settling into Everton's midfield.

of the national side's five-year-old unbeaten Under-21 squad due to a shortage of cash. 'When we played there was one team and you were expected to perform on a world-class stage when you hadn't had any previous international background,' adds Marley. 'Now they are progressing into the seniors with 25 caps at younger ages, they are going to be better prepared.' It is the kind of experience elite Scandinavian teenagers have been enjoying for around twenty years. Sweden and Norway's sixteen-year-olds went head-to-head in their first international in 1986 – a good twelve years before England had even set up an Under-16 squad.

Why were England slow to follow suit? According to Lopez, European football's governing body UEFA wanted national associations to take control of women's football in their countries as early as 1971 – a year before the Women's Football Association set up an official England team. Many European countries took up that clarion call, but it took the English FA another twenty-two years to make the step and fully take over the running of the women's game from the hard-working but cash-strapped WFA. It was a costly delay. 'It is interesting to note that those nations that did fully, and positively, integrate the women's game back in the 1970s, such as Sweden, Denmark, Norway and Germany, are among the world leaders today,' observes Lopez.

The FA looked to make amends for its slow-coach approach in 1997 when, under the direction of Howard Wilkinson, Kelly Simmons and England boss Ted Copeland, it launched the Talent Development Plan for women's football. Looking to the success of Millwall Lionesses' Centre of Excellence, the plan saw the FA give its backing to twenty such centres for ten- to sixteen-year-old girls and launched two youth sides, the Under-18s, and the Under-16s, which came on stream a year later. The aim was to create a 'Player Pathway' that gives youngsters at school, junior and youth club level the chance to hone their skills before moving in to the England youth set-up if they have the talent. By 2007, two additional youth sides had been formed and the centres of excellence numbered fifty-two.

The Women's Sports Foundation says the centres are 'supporting' England's rise in the world rankings, but it is rooting for even more. 'There remains a postcode lottery for starting, staying and excelling in women and girls' football,' the group wrote in a memorandum to the 2006 House of Commons Select Committee. 'Greater choice and a diversity of opportunities through an increased number of clubs, increased number of female coaches and improved facilities is critical for building upon progress made to date'. The FA's Trevor Brooking hopes the development plan will pay off in the long term. 'What we want and what we are starting to get is a good structure in place so that if you can identify the talented young girls you've to try and encourage them to come through the system,' he says. It is a system that has been augmented by new youth competitions such as the inaugural Under-17 World Cup in 2008, all of which Hope Powell sees as motivation for budding youngsters:

> Those are things that the younger players can aspire to and [which make them] more conscientious about their game... All the squads, all the players, right down to fifteen, are given personalised conditioning programmes... we have regional testing centres and it gives the young player some aspiration at fifteen to become a Kelly Smith at twenty-one.

Carney, who is incidentally rated by Smith as another English footballer capable of a FIFA Women's World Player of the Year nomination, is the epitome of this pyramid progression. The Midlander has gone from playing schoolgirl football at Solihull College mini soccer centre, to running out for Solihull Borough girls' team, training at Coventry then Birmingham centres of excellence, getting stuck into youth and senior league action with Birmingham City, playing international matches at every level in the England set-up and enrolling on a scholarship at Loughborough. Without that last option, England might have seen Carney lured overseas as offers from American universities rolled in shortly after she arrived at the NPDC. But home-loving Carney was content at her new college and both the Blues and her national side were able to keep hold of their player.

Given Carney's Wayne Rooney-style rise to fame in the Euros, Birmingham City were happy to still have the FA's Young Player of the Year on their roster in August 2005. Birmingham had not only lost out on sponsorship and seen London-based players Alex Scott and Rachel Yankey depart; they had also seen Carney elevated to most-wanted status. But the star winger felt a responsibility to stick by the club she joined as a twelve-year-old from Solihull Borough:

> At the back of the Euros I had a few offers saying come and play for me… It wasn't in my heart really. When you've been with the team who have made you who you are, I thought it would be disrespectful to leave and I didn't feel comfortable with a move at that time.

Birmingham had done well to play their part in making Carney the player she had become. When she first joined up with the Blues at the urging of then Solihull College sports development officer Rachel Pavlou, the Birmingham City men's-team fan was just as interested in dancing as playing football. Unlike many of her contemporaries in the England team, who were kicking a ball before they could even walk, Carney was dancing the light fantastic well before she touched a football at home with her sister Sarah, who later became Solihull Ladies team manager. 'I did dancing from two till about fifteen,' she says. 'I was probably more of a dancer than a footballer. I used to go dancing Tuesdays and Saturdays and I'd play football on a Saturday morning and rush straight to dancing, then I'd have dancing on Sunday as well.' Smearing herself in fake tan in preparation for performances of hip hop, rock 'n' roll and disco – solo, in a doubles partnership and with her troupe The Knock – in places like youth dance mecca Blackpool meant Carney would occasionally bring more colour to her Saturday games than she meant to. 'She'd go on the pitch on a Saturday and they'd say, "You been on your holiday?" It was like November or something and they used to laugh,' says her mum Marie. 'And if it was raining, you'd be horrified because it starts streaking a little bit.'

Dancing the weekend away was all well and good while Carney was making her way up Birmingham City's ranks alongside fellow first-team prospect Eniola Aluko. But when professional footballer and Birmingham manager Marcus Bignot offered Carney a break into the first team and Sunday football in the 2001/02 season, the player had to rethink her priorities. 'Marcus was like, "You're going to start on Sunday" and I said, I can't come Marcus, gotta go to dancing,' she recalls. It wasn't quite the reaction the professional footballer was expecting from a fourteen-year-old who had just been told she was about to get a shot at the big time but Bignot was impressed by her dedication. 'It was refreshing to see she tried to combine the two,' he says. 'Kaz was dancing as soon as she could walk and had to juggle the two.' Bignot still kept his eye on the prize, though, and was ready to take Carney when push came to shove and the teenager realised her future lay in dancing past defences not jiving for judges:

> I'd kind of switched my focus away from dance… I just went through the motions really. You know in football you say 'train as you play', I didn't really dance as I'd dance, I just kind of went through it and people got better than me and it just worked out that way.

There was no going through the motions once Carney put her mind to her football. That season, the player was on the fringe of the squad that won promotion to the National Division and faced Fulham in the League Cup final, where they lost 7-1 to the professionals. Carney was on the verge of breaking into the national set-up too, a call-up for a youth friendly against an English Universities side confirming early predictions. 'I think a few people had said, "Oh she's going to play for England",' says Carney. 'I thought, well I am going to do it one day, I'm determined to do it and did it.' Finding the net against the university students helped Carney achieve her dream. The net bulged twice more in six Under-17 appearances and by the time she was sixteen Carney had landed a place at Loughborough alongside the likes of Amanda Barr and Casey Stoney.

Free-scoring Barr, or 'Munch' as she was known in the football world, caught the nation's eye when she netted 11 times in 18 games for the Under-18s. Her last-gasp goal for the seniors against Iceland in 2002 saw England into the play-off final for the World Cup 2003, which they eventually lost to France. The PE and sports science BTEC student was just as goal hungry on the domestic front, winning two successive FA golden boot awards while leading the line at Charlton Athletic. Her England colleague, the former Arsenal treble winner and FA Cup-winning Charlton skipper Stoney, had been thrown into the cut and thrust of women's football as a youngster with Chelsea. Having rejected cricket and a place on the British korfball team to make it into top-flight football, she set her sights on England after watching highlights on Channel 4 as a youngster. She achieved her dream aged eighteen, making her debut for England alongside Rachel Unitt in front of thousands of roaring fans against France at the Velodrome in Marseille. As a versatile defender capable of playing every which way across the back four, Stoney had, like Barr, been a squad regular if sporadic starter ever since. Carney, who was yet to even taste senior international football when she arrived at Loughborough, was buoyed by the presence of the two England seniors. 'When I first came I was so nervous and I'd be in front of goal and kick the ball over the bar,' she says. 'I thought, I'm a bit out of my depth here, but all of a sudden it just clicked.' Fall into place it certainly did, with call-ups to the England Under-19s followed by promotion to the newly formed Under-21s along with fellow Blues Laura Bassett, Faye Cardin, Shelly Cox and Vicky Gallagher. 'The 17s and 19s was great because I just played football, enjoyed it and was working my way up the ladder,' she says. By then, Carney also felt she fitted in with the regime at Loughborough where she had friends who understood the game and mixed with other inspirational athletes. 'One time I was in the canteen and Jonny Wilkinson was there so you do feel a bit special,' she says. 'Everyone is striving

Karen Carney has had to learn the media ropes pretty quickly after all the recognition she has received.

towards being the best in their sport so it's what you want to aim to do.'

This degree of dedication would be needed at club level too as spring 2006 came into view. Birmingham had triumphed in the County Cup but endured a tough time in the league. With their other big-name players gone, Carney was the glue that held the side together. It was not a feeling that sat easily with one so young. She says:

> I think it was probably more pressure on myself that I gave. I was only eighteen and I thought, I've come off the Euros, I've got to carry this team now and I didn't have to. I didn't have to do anything, I just had to work hard. But it wasn't nice for me. I was probably a bit low and it was a really difficult season – I was injured for maybe three or four months of it and it was difficult.

Carney would move on to Arsenal once the season ended and she felt 'everyone was safe and sound' at her beloved Birmingham.

1 Hope Powell ponders her team selection for a tough World Cup qualifying campaign.

2 4-0 up already and Rachel Yankey prepares to take another corner against Hungary in Tapolca.

3 *Above:* Kelly Smith and Jody Handley run in as Fara Williams slots home from the spot for the record thirteenth goal against Hungary.

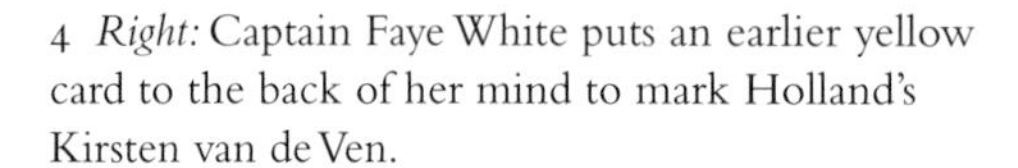

4 *Right:* Captain Faye White puts an earlier yellow card to the back of her mind to mark Holland's Kirsten van de Ven.

5 Young Holland fans enjoy the game against England while it is still goal-less in Zwolle.

6 Anita Asante replaces Vicky Exley (4) in Holland to make her first qualification appearance.

7 *Above:* Local fans turn out to cheer on England against France at Blackburn's Ewood Park.

8 *Right:* Kelly Smith goes home happy after picking up the Player of the Match award for the friendly against Iceland in Norwich.

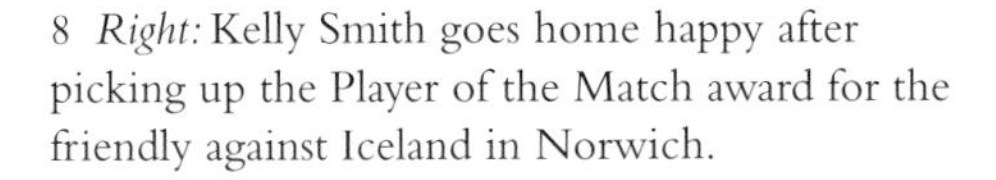

9 Goalkeeper Rachel Brown joins in the England huddle before turning in a Player of the Match performance.

10 Norwegian referee Bente Skogvang asks Rachel Yankey and Anne-Laure Casseleux to keep it cool while France captain Sonia Bompastor (8) watches on.

11 *Above:* One half down, forty-five minutes left to play in the grudge match with France at Ewood Park.

12 *Right:* Casey Stoney considers her options as England battle to overcome France.

13 The Blackburn boys are out in force for the crunch tie against France at Ewood.

14 England prepare to take on Austria at Gillingham's Priestfield Stadium with captain Faye White back leading the team. From left to right, back row: Kelly Smith, Fara Williams, Rachel Brown, Katie Chapman, Rachel Unitt, Lindsay Johnson. Front row: Rachel Yankey, Mary Phillip, Amanda Barr, Karen Carney, Faye White.

15 *Above left:* Karen Carney looks to receive the ball under pressure from Austria's Nina Aigner.

16 *Above right:* Sue Smith shows speed and concentration as she flies down the left wing.

17 *Above left:* Rachel Unitt pauses for reflection as England struggle to break Austria down.

18 *Above right:* Sue Smith adds to her tally with a goal against Austria to the delight of Rachel Unitt (3) and Kelly Smith (10).

19 Vicky Exley (16) and Jo Potter (15) warm up their shooting boots.

20 Fara Williams (8) is poised to follow up but Kelly Smith easily buries her penalty.

21 *Above left:* Left-back Rachel Unitt joins the attack as England take on Holland at The Valley.

22 *Above right:* Rachel Yankey shields the ball from Holland's Liesbeth Migchelsen.

23 Rachel Brown (left) listens intently as Mary Phillip addresses journalists at a press conference.

24 Eniola Aluko (6) and Vicky Exley (10) stay primed as Alex Scott (centre) goes on the attack in a warm-up session.

25 Stand-in captain Mary Phillip (centre, facing) must rally the troops in the all-important final game against France in Rennes.

26 The England team's friends and families arrive for the match at the Stade de la Route de Lorient in Rennes.

27 Skipper for the day Mary Phillip leads the team out against France followed by Rachel Brown, Kelly Smith, Eniola Aluko et al.

28 The France team look confident ahead of their must-win match against England. From left to right, back row: Hoda Lattaf, Sandrine Soubeyrand, Laure Lepailleur, Laëtitia Tonazzi, Laura Georges, Elise Bussaglia. Front row: Marinette Pichon, Sarah Bouhaddi, Sandrine Dusang, Sonia Bompastor, Anne-Laure Casseleux.

29 England show no nerves despite a stadium packed with over 19,000 French fans. From left to right, back row: Rachel Yankey, Rachel Brown, Rachel Unitt, Katie Chapman, Mary Phillip, Karen Carney. Front row: Fara Williams, Alex Scott, Eniola Aluko, Kelly Smith, Anita Asante.

30 *Above left:* The fans along the left wing are treated to some good attacking play by Kelly Smith.

31 *Above right:* France's Anne-Laure Casseleux puts in a challenge as Katie Chapman attacks.

32 *Above left:* They've done it! Eniola Aluko turns to celebrate their goal with the England fans.

33 *Above right:* With England 1-0 up from an own goal, Fara Williams stakes a claim for the goal.

34 Eniola Aluko (9), Fara Williams (8) and Katie Chapman (4) are flying high after holding France to a 1-1 draw.

35 Rachel Yankey (left) and Karen Carney (right) flank their injured club and country captain Faye White as the three celebrate in Rennes.

36 Katie Chapman spots her family amongst the travelling England fans.

37 Travelling all that way has been worth it – to witness England's dramatic final game.

38 *Above left:* Lindsay Johnson spots a friendly face in the crowd as Jody Handley (14) joins in the celebrations.

39 *Above right:* Striker Marinette Pichon is consoled by old teammate Kelly Smith after France fail to reach what would have been her last World Cup.

40 The watching snappers home in as Karen Carney is hugged by teammate Katie Chapman.

41 The changing room at the Stade de la Route de Lorient gets a soaking in champagne as the England team celebrate qualification.

Believing it was a good move for their loyal charge, the club gave her their wholehearted backing. 'We practically drove her down the motorway,' says Birmingham City chairman Steve Shipway. Carney would drive back up it to support her old teammates whenever she got the chance and more often than not, her mum Marie would volunteer to flip burgers in their food stand to help out. 'If I can I like to go because it was probably one of the hardest decisions Karen has had to make,' Marie says. 'They were very good to me, especially when I was ill and they've been very good to Karen.'

In March 2006, however, Carney was still running out for the Blues while working towards World Cup qualification with England. Looming on the horizon was the crunch tie against France, the nation that had shattered England's dreams by beating them in the World Cup 2003 play-off final while Carney was still a schoolgirl. But first, England wanted to keep a confidence-boosting five-game unbeaten run going by seeing off the Icelandic national team. Trundling through the turnstiles at Norwich FC's compact ground are 9,616 supporters – around 1,500 more than have ever turned out to watch England in a friendly since the national team was formed in 1972. Hope Powell puts the surge in numbers down to making friends in the Euros. 'We won a lot of new fans,' she says. Carney won plenty of new fans too and with the Euros still fresh in supporters' minds, there's a clear sense of excitement in the air whenever the winger picks up possession. Which she does in the first minute, whipping in a cross which Fara Williams gets a head to but nudges wide of the post. England, shorn of skipper Faye White as preparation for her suspension in the next game, feature bustling midfielder Katie Chapman at the centre of defence alongside Carney's old college friend Casey Stoney in the right-back position she commands for Charlton. They are soon tested, dependable stand-in Chapman forced to concede a corner to stop Margrét Vidarsdóttir in her tracks after a cute pass from Hólmfrídur Magnúsdóttir. But Rachel Brown's makeshift defence has the experience to hold firm and it is her opposite number who is soon under the cosh as Carney, Kelly Smith and Rachel Yankey pile the pressure on at the other end. A blocked shot from Smith sees Williams follow up with a neat turn and shot for which Thóra Helgadóttir has to make a diving save. The keeper needs to stay on her mettle as goal-getter Eni Aluko gets a touch on a powerful cross from Smith in the twenty-fifth minute. Chapman may be back in defence, but she rushes forward to bolster the attack as England win a corner. The athletic Chapman's effort is almost rewarded as she comes close with a header from a Yankey corner on thirty-four minutes but her contact is off and the ball sails over the bar. Kelly Smith reveals the full extent of her talents as she finds space on the edge of the box to send in a strong left-foot shot that is only kept out by the crossbar. Iceland are defending stoutly, though, and Helgadóttir proves her agility as she gets a hand to Aluko's shot from a dangerous Yankey cross just before half-time. England are dominant but need to turn that strength into goals.

They give it a go after the break, Anita Asante getting in on the attack to unleash a decent effort before Chapman shoots just wide. On the hour, Margrét Vidarsdóttir breaks away again and her shot forces a great save from substitute goalkeeper Siobhan Chamberlain. But it is England who wrap up the tie as the clock ticks down. In a story-book finish, Rachel Unitt whips in a cross from the left that is deftly diverted by Carney's forehead. It is the only goal of the game and it makes her mother's day just over ten minutes from time.

'I'm not a header of the ball but I was told to give it a go so I did,' grins Carney afterwards. Sitting alongside her in Norwich's shiny silver-walled press room, manager Powell is grateful to her England pupil for using her head. But she also acknowledges that the match has taught her team a lesson in the need for clinical finishing. 'We possibly overplayed at times but created lots of opportunities,' she says. 'We do need to be more clinical.' Powell's words would prove prophetic in England's next crucial tie – at home to rivals France, less than three weeks later.

New Friends, Old Foes

After the diversion of Iceland came the crunch World Cup qualifier against France and a return to the scene of England's Euro 2005 agony – Ewood Park. Having been unexpectedly beaten by the Dutch in September, the French were on the back foot, trailing England by three points. But it was not just the French who were licking their wounds ahead of this meeting, England were too. Not simply because this game was to be played out on the ground that saw Powell's group eliminated from the Euros. More because it was against the country that had broken English hearts by beating them in the two-legged play-off for the fifth European place in the World Cup 2003 finals.

Spurred on from the stands by their male counterparts, the Arsenal FC players Patrick Vieira, Robert Pires and Sylvain Wiltord, France had eked out a 1-0 win over England in the home leg at Selhurst Park in October 2002. As England were shorn of the injured Kelly Smith and pregnant Katie Chapman, it was down to eighteen-year-old Fara Williams to boss the midfield. Twisting and turning her way through the French defence at will, Williams tried to do just that. But her efforts amounted to nothing when talismanic striker Marinette Pichon silenced the home crowd with the winner fifteen minutes from time. All hopes of making the finals were unequivocally dashed when the French hit the same scoreline again less than a month later, skipper Corinne Diacre bagging the only goal of the game to book her country's ticket to the World Cup. Williams remembers that defeat in front of over 23,000 screaming fans in St Etienne like it was yesterday. 'Their fans were jumping on cages when they beat us,' she recalls, 'it was horrible.'

Ten of the World Cup 2007 qualification squad witnessed that night in France. Not surprisingly, a steely determination not to suffer a similar fate in this home tie was at the forefront of their minds. 'France are a very good side and are favourites to get out of this group,' said Hope Powell beforehand. 'Our job is to make sure that doesn't happen, it will be a big test but one we will relish.' England's preparations to pass that test this time, however, extended beyond the purely physical and tactical. In the aftermath of their World Cup 2003 play-off disappointment, Powell recruited a psychologist in a bid to turn her team of nearly women into the most mentally robust group in the world. With England having let in just one goal in three qualification victories, it was a ploy that seemed to be working.

Williams and her England room-mate Rachel Brown, a substitute in St Etienne but a key player in this qualification campaign, certainly seemed to think the changes had made a difference. According to Williams, the England she first knew had never been overly disappointed at losing to so-called 'bigger' football nations. Now, Williams insists, Powell's group have the self belief to 'grind out that extra ten minutes or per cent for each other'. Why? 'The psychologist is the difference,' chips in the keeper as the two take time out in the offices of Everton FC's community department at Goodison Park where Williams is a women and girls' development coach, and qualified teacher Brown manages their healthy school bus.

Quite how many footballers would include sheets of A4 paper, pictures from magazines and magic markers as vital parts of their kit is anyone's guess. But for Williams, Brown and their colleagues on the England women's team, they have become as essential as shin pads and socks. Inspirational messages and pictures are penned, cut out and stuck on bits of paper around the changing room to remind the players of their hopes and aspirations. A photo of Chelsea centre-back John Terry can be found above Rachel Unitt's changing-room

A confident Fara Williams looks relaxed after an Everton victory.

peg. While the more austere image of a sergeant major and the word 'communicator' inspires Brown to remain strong out on the field. 'I have a mental pre-match preparation which I take very seriously,' says Brown. 'And if a goal goes in, I've got a recovery strategy and these are little things that have been introduced to me by the psychologist.' Others such as Williams ink key words on to handmade wristbands. The words 'breathe', 'relax' and 'composure', along with a smiley face usually feature on the midfielder's wrist come match day. Judging by the gentle joshing the two Everton colleagues indulge in, those key words are not just required out on the field of play.

Rolling her eyes at the antics of one of the few England players to have acquired an agent post-Euros, Williams recalls how Brown is a notoriously messy room-mate who regularly tests her composure to the full. 'Browny is very untidy,' announces Williams in a machine gun-fast London accent. 'She used to go to breakfast and I would clean the room and she would come back and say, "Oh, has the maid been?" and I'd say, no I cleaned up for you.' Thankfully, another element introduced to the team by their psychologist has been the ability to handle criticism and admit your failings. According to Williams, team meetings now see the entire squad ready to stand up and be counted. 'Before, you would hide things from your team-mates and not be open enough to say I'm struggling or be able to take criticism,' she says. Brown adds, 'Now we know how people like to be spoken to and how they react.'

When it came to mental toughness, Williams needed all she could muster – the midfielder had assumed the unenviable job as England's penalty taker. Walking up to place the ball in front of Denmark's goal at Ewood Park during the Euros, Williams had blocked out the 14,695 strong crowd to coolly dispatch it into the back of the net. She had done the same against Austria, Hungary and Holland in this World Cup 2007 qualification campaign and her goalscoring prowess would come into play right up until the final whistle in September 2006. It was all in a day's work for a player who burst into the England set-up as a fourteen-year-old in an Under-16 development squad and scored on her full debut for the seniors less than a month after her eighteenth birthday. That sliced free-kick in a World Cup qualifier against Portugal in front of almost 9,000 supporters at Portsmouth's Fratton Park confirmed her talent as a dead-ball specialist. Within months, Williams was being dubbed by FA website scribes as playing like a 'female Joe Cole' when she flew the flag for England seniors in their bid to reach the World Cup 2003. It was a world away from the west London housing estate streets where Williams took her very first spot kick.

Then, a seven-year-old Williams would knock a ball against a wall with her sister Tara while enviously listening to the roars emanating from Stamford Bridge. 'My family were Chelsea mad,' says Williams. 'I remember they went to a game and me and my sister were sat at my nan's and we could hear the crowd and we really wanted to go.' On their return, the Williams sisters made the streets their pitch with a goal drawn on the wall. The brickwork at Williams' old primary school in Battersea also took a hammering as head teacher

Brian Jones doled out lessons in two-footed play to the England prospect. In the meantime, the youngster had finally made it through the Stamford Bridge turnstiles, handing over a mere £3 with her brothers Adam and Aaron to watch a six-goal thriller against Luton. It was a gripping match that had the Williams clan running home to play with even more conviction than before.

Evading mixed-team bans, Williams went on to play for her secondary school's boys' team – in goal. The keeper soon cast off her gloves to get stuck into the midfield role she now plays with England. Putting in a Player of the Tournament performance at a local festival – taking the gong ahead of scores of disgruntled boys – Williams caught the eye of a Fulham scout and soon found herself running out for the Cottagers' youth team. Wearing the white of Fulham only lasted a year, though. Williams' Blues mad Uncle Neil urged his niece to team up with their beloved Chelsea and despite catching the wrong bus and arriving late and flustered for her trial, she was in. Williams was in with England too, landing call-ups to the new youth development squad, before making her Under-18 debut as a substitute against Moldova in a UEFA Championship qualifying tournament in Shropshire. England romped to a whopping 15-0 victory.

Having England come calling was rather a shock to the teenager, who, like Sue Smith and others before her, was oblivious to England women. 'I didn't know England had a women's team,' she says. 'Then I saw England play Scotland on the telly and Vicky Exley came on as a sub and I remember thinking she's just a kid, I want to do that.' To make that step up a reality, Williams had to leave her beloved Chelsea, who played in the Southern Division, for a team in the Premier League's National Division, one tier above. 'I didn't want to leave there,' says Williams. 'But Hope said you'll never get into the senior team until you play at a higher level.' It was a difficult decision. Chelsea had come agonisingly close to promotion to the National Division that season, thanks in most part to the 30 goals Williams had bagged from midfield. But they missed out by a point and with her heart set on England, Williams jumped on the train with her Chelsea colleague Eartha Pond to check out the National Division's London-based sides. They unexpectedly came home from their first try-out as Charlton players even though Williams says the two had meant to check out Vic Akers and his Arsenal Ladies side as well. 'We'd promised Vic we would go and have a look at what they had to offer and I was gutted, we never even went,' Williams recalls. Although she would later return to the Addicks, Arsenal Academy student Pond switched to the Gunners a few months later after her journey across London from college to training took its toll. 'I had to travel for about four hours and leave lessons early,' recalls Pond. Once her studies were done, the defender returned to Charlton. There, she teamed up again with her old friend Williams, who had stayed put having broken into England seniors within two months of arriving in south-east London.

That season, seven goals in 20 league and cup appearances earned Williams the accolades of Charlton Player of the Year and FA Young Player of the Year. Shrugging off a fractured metatarsal, she went on to compete in the scorching heat for England in the Under-19 World Cup 2002 in Canada. England made it to the last eight but were sent packing by hosts and eventual finalists Canada, who beat them 6-2 in the quarter-finals to the delight of 23,595 screaming fans. Hope Powell's assistant Brent Hills made sure the England players took more than a suntan home from that tournament, however. 'I was told in the Under-19 World Cup by Brent that to improve you have to look at the best players in the world, take from their game and put it into yours,' she says. 'I used to think I was Maradona but I've learnt you have to take one or two touches, get it out of your feet and play.'

All that playing took its toll on the growing teenager who had been involved in sport most of her life, however. Williams suffered a stress fracture of the back the following season but gritted her teeth and still managed a dozen run-outs for her club. She wished she had not bothered when it came to the showpiece FA Cup final in May

2003. Fulham were on for the treble and showed little mercy against Charlton at Selhurst Park. With his side 2-0 down, Keith Boanas threw Williams into the fray but the substitute inadvertently sealed the Addicks' fate, heading Rachel Unitt's corner into her own net just three minutes after taking to the pitch.

Come July, a revitalised Williams had shrugged off injury and that own-goal blow to lead the England Under-19s in the eight-nation European Championship in Germany. Featuring soon-to-be senior teammates Anita Asante, Alex Scott, Jo Potter and sixteen-year-old Eniola Aluko, the team recorded an impressive victory over Sweden – their skipper capping a Woman of the Match performance in the eighty-ninth minute with a blistering volley from twenty-five yards out to seal a 2-1 win. Williams went on to score once more as England beat Italy but she could not steer the side all the way to the final and they fell 2-0 to France in the semi. At least her return to full fitness was complete. Charlton reaped the rewards the following season as they lifted the League Cup with victory over Fulham thanks to a single goal by Emma Coss.

The Addicks were on target for the treble that year, but it was not to be. Williams and her club-mates experienced their second 3-0 FA Cup final defeat on the trot – this time to a Julie Fleeting-inspired Arsenal – and they saw the Gunners pip them to the title when they beat Fulham at Highbury on the last day of the season. It would be Williams' last with Charlton. After three years working with Addicks' boss Keith Boanas, the midfield dynamo switched to Everton. Boanas was sad to learn he had lost the player that he and his partner, goalkeeper Pauline Cope, had taken under their wing. 'I used to drive her to training and she would come to dinner with me and Copes,' he says. 'I just wish I could have worked with her longer and made her an even better player.' That task fell on Mo Marley's shoulders, however, as Williams opted to make the move north. Arriving at Everton's first training night, the southerner soon discovered that life with the amateur side was a far cry from her time with the Addicks. 'At Charlton, I used to turn up for training and the kit would be piled up, ironed and folded,' she says. 'Here, there are people training in Liverpool shorts and I wear my Chelsea shorts. But on the pitch we play for each other.'

Joining in with the camaraderie were her England colleagues Rachel Unitt, Rachel Brown, Jody Handley and Lindsay Johnson. Striker Handley was in her second spell with the Merseyside club, having returned after three seasons at Doncaster Belles where she had formed a vibrant strike force with then England skipper Karen Walker. Handley replaced her hotshot colleague when she took her England bow – coming on for Walker at half-time in an England friendly against Nigeria at Norwich City FC in July 2002. Handley played from first whistle two months later, turning out as England defeated Iceland in the World Cup 2003 play-off semi-final and she notched up her first international goal thirteen months later in a 2-2 draw against Russia in chilly Moscow. Returning to Everton in 2004, Handley would help new teammate Williams realise her dream of a third successive FA Cup final the following May. The striker was among the goalscorers when Everton cruised past Arsenal 3-0 in the semi-final of the competition at Southport FC to book the club's first FA Cup final in sixteen years. Ironically, the side they would meet at Upton Park for the prestigious tie was Charlton. Williams' England colleague Lindsay Johnson would be marked out as player of the game in that contest. Former Liverpool and England Under-21 defender 'Johno' was a relative newcomer to both the Everton and England senior set-ups by May 2005, but had made her mark in the Algarve Cup that March as England kept a clean sheet in all four games. She also became irreplaceable at the heart of the Toffees' defence that season, as the FA Club of the Year claimed third spot in the league, conceding 24 goals in 18 games.

Everton in the Community football development officer Johnson was due to celebrate her twenty-fifth birthday six days after the FA Cup final, but she would do so without a winners' medal in her hands. A jubilant Boanas and his Addicks made it third time lucky when Williams' former England Under-19 teammate Eni Aluko

Everton teammates from left to right: Becky Easton, Jody Handley, Rachel Brown, Lindsay Johnson and Rachel Unitt are all glammed up to celebrate their Club of the Year award in 2005.

knocked in the only goal. 'I lost again for the third year in a row,' Williams shrugs. It was a feeling her Everton colleague Rachel Brown could empathise with as she nursed a knee injury on the sidelines. As a fifteen-year-old Liverpool player, the keeper had lost out to Hope Powell's Croydon in the 1996 FA Cup final. It was a low point in a whirlwind season that had seen Brown elevated to first-choice keeper at the Merseyside club within weeks of her arrival. 'She was just flung in at the deep end,' recalls her then team-mate Karen Burke. 'She was only a baby.' It was typical of Brown not to duck the challenge.

While Williams was keeping goal for her new secondary school boys' team, a teenage Brown was arriving in America with her keeper gloves in one hand and a letter of introduction in the other. Having agreed to help out at a US soccer school in Alabama, the lass from Burnley had finished her GCSEs and promptly hopped on a plane to America's Deep South. 'I went the day after my last exam and stayed with a family I'd never met before,' she laughs. It was not the first, nor would it be the last time that Brown would venture into the unknown. Having caught the football bug while watching the men's Italia '90 World Cup on the TV, Browny would practise in her nan's back yard during summer holiday visits to Blackpool and at home with boys' team Bank Hall United. Progressing to Accrington Stanley as a mere twelve-year-old threw Brown into the world of women's football. But she still kept up with the lads when, a year later, the boyish youngster with bobbed hair the colour of cotton wool persuaded her parents Tim and Margaret to pack her off to London for a goalkeeping course. Brown was the only girl among fifty keepers at that week-long Bob Wilson training camp but she still managed to impress the powers that be. The offer of a Liverpool Ladies trial promptly dropped on to the doorstep of her Burnley home upon her return and a month or so after her fifteenth birthday, Brown was walking into uncharted territory once more.

National Division side Liverpool were literally leagues above Accrington Stanley so when she signed for the club, Brown thought she was about to serve a long apprenticeship. No such luck. Veteran Tracey Davidson left Liverpool shortly after the teenage rookie arrived and Brown was called up to play before she had even fastened the straps on her gloves. 'I was planning on being mentored for a couple of years,' she admits. Within days, Brown had Marieanne Spacey and Arsenal bearing down on her at Anfield and by the season's end, Brown was walking out in front of over 2,000 supporters at Millwall's New Den as one of the youngest players ever to take part in an FA Women's Cup final. Hope Powell was captain of the Croydon squad that defeated Liverpool on penalties that April day in 1996. Powell cancelled out Karen Burke's opening goal and after 120 minutes of football had ended 1-1, Brown was faced with a nerve-racking penalty shoot-out. The teenager pulled out all the stops to save one spot kick but Croydon kept their cool to win the cup. It was a bitter defeat but the kind of performance that would bring her under England's radar. 'She had enormous potential,' the then

The articulate Rachel Brown has become a glamorous face of the England team.

national side manager Ted Copeland recalls. 'She was young and immature as a player but technically she was probably one of the best goalkeepers in the squad.'

By the time she was sixteen, Brown was putting her technique to the test and joining seventeen-year-old Sue Smith on the pitch at Preston as England played out that 6-4 friendly defeat to Germany. Neither player had acquired the glammed-up and media-savvy image they present to the world today. But then again, they were both so wet behind the ears that, like many of their contemporaries, neither had even realised there was an England team full stop. 'I remember these girls coming back to Liverpool with England shorts on and talking about England and the World Cup,' Brown recalls. 'They had been to Sweden '95 and I was like, wow, is there an England team? A year later I was in the squad.'

Eighteen months on from that match against Germany and Brown was packing her size nine gloves and heading out into the world on her own again. Scholarship offers arrived thick and fast after the summer school outing a couple of years previously and Brown opted for the University of Alabama. It was a world away from her home town Burnley but it did not matter. 'I'm not homesick,' she says. 'I've always been independent so I've always been fine to just get on with things, being in America helped with that.' Unhappy with life at Alabama, Brown nonchalantly switched to Pittsburgh in the north-east of the country. The new kid on the block soon won over the Pittsburgh Panthers fans and the league, grabbing Big East Goalkeeper of the Year plaudits and holding a university record for letting in the fewest goals in a season. Throughout it all, Brown remained in contention for England, keeping regular no.1 Pauline Cope on her toes. 'I learnt so much from her,' Brown says of her mentor. 'She never felt threatened, we always worked our hardest for each other. I pushed her and we'd notice things about each other's game and help each other.' Brown's education with Cope was allowed to continue because the FA were prepared to fly her back for games and her university allowed her to take exams in hotel rooms. It had its downsides, though. 'It sounds glamorous but it was so tiring,' she says. 'I'd be away for a week so would have to catch up and take tests that I'd missed. By the time I caught up we were going away again.'

After four and a half years in the US, Brown was returning home again, this time to apply for a teaching degree and elite sports scholarship at Liverpool John Moores University alongside the likes of Olympic gymnast Beth Tweddle. With her course not due to start until September, the twenty-two-year-old threw herself into coaching under-12 girls in Lancashire centres of excellence and playing in the thick of the English National Division. Signing for Everton on her return that Christmas 2002, she found herself mired in a relegation battle. But the Merseyside club had signed England veteran

Sammy Britton along with Brown and Everton survived by the skin of their teeth, a 1-0 win over Southampton Saints in mid-March moving them out of the drop zone. That job done, Brown was left waiting for her teaching course to start. Marking off the days did not sit well with the player but a phone call from an England and former Liverpool teammate ensured the shot stopper was not twiddling her thumbs for long:

> I was sat at home waiting for September and Karen Burke rang me up and said, 'Hiya Browny, what are you up to, do you want to come and play in Iceland?' I was like, 'Yeah,' and she said, 'I'm here now, we need a goalie.' I was like, 'Oh cool, when's that for?' She said, 'Well we've got a game day after tomorrow so can you come tomorrow?' So I just packed up and went the next morning.

Playing for ÍBV in Vestmannaeyjar off the south coast of Iceland opened Brown's eyes to new training moves and ways of moving a team too. Rather than piling into the team minibus for away games, the players at ÍBV flew from the volcanic islands to the mainland. It was a quick flight but Brown could see the controls from her seat in the tiny aircraft and set her mind on co-piloting the plane. 'You could see the pilot and Rach was like, "Give us a go, give us a go" and he was just like, "Go on then",' laughs Burke. 'It was madness, she was just turning around saying, "I'm flying" and we were saying, "Keep your eyes forward, we're going to crash".' They were joking, of course, but Brown did make an impact with her safe hands and sparky personality and was invited back the following summer. She returned, but that season was all about coaching and cutting grass. Brown had suffered a serious knee ligament injury while keeping goal for Everton in January 2004 and so her duties out in Iceland were to coach the goalies and keep the grass trim alongside teammates Sammy Britton and Burke. 'It would be torrential rain and we'd still be out with our strimmers just laughing our heads off and stinking of petrol,' recalls Burke. 'It was hilarious,' agrees Brown.

Taking on the role of goalkeeping coach allows Rachel Brown to pass on her expertise to emerging talent.

If the happy-go-lucky keeper was to remain in England contention, however, she knew the fun had to end and the hard work begin. In April that year, England keeper Cope announced her sudden retirement from the international scene. The Charlton player's decision to call it a day after a career that garnered 60 caps effectively turned the quest to become first-choice shot-stopper at the 2005 Euros into a two-horse race between Brown and Leanne Hall. The Fulham keeper had made an impressive return having broken her leg in a fifth round FA Cup match for Leeds against Aston Villa the previous season. After her recuperation in Iceland, Brown needed to pull off a similar comeback to put herself in contention for the Euros. A combination of new-found visualisation techniques courtesy of the team psychologist and over twelve months' hard graft out on the pitch and in the gym meant Browny was ready in time. By then, though, Birmingham City's talented keeper Jo Fletcher was also making a bid for the no.1 shirt. The new girl had debuted alongside Karen Carney in a 4-1 win over Italy in February 2005 and went on to keep clean sheets against Mexico, Portugal and China in the Algarve Cup. It was enough to land the twenty-four-year-old a place between the sticks in the opening games of the Euros. But Powell told the rival goalies that she would also be throwing Brown into the fray. Her chance came in front of 25,694 screaming fans in England's final Euro 2005 match against Sweden. That 1-0 defeat at Ewood Park saw the home side miss out on Euro glory in their own back yard, but the keeper, who retained the no.1 shirt ahead of Hall after Fletcher ruled herself out of contention by joining the army, was determined to see a better outcome when she stood between the sticks at Blackburn Rovers' ground in March 2006.

Around 6,000 tickets had been sold in advance of the tie on Mother's Day and a further 6,000 supporters piled through the gates to watch the game that could determine the rest of England's campaign. There was a party atmosphere around the ground, with a mums and daughters soccer skills challenge and a tournament for local Asian girls being played out during the day. In the dressing room, however, there was a slightly edgier atmosphere, enhanced by the knowledge that France had overtaken Sweden to sit fifth in the world rankings and were coming into the game off the back of a fourth-placed finish in the Algarve Cup invitational competition in Portugal. 'Okay, they were really nervous this week if the truth be known,' said Powell after the match, her record-breaking seventy-first in charge of the national side. 'They were looking forward to it [but there was] a bit of nerves, you know, the occasion and the team we're playing against, who are ranked a lot higher than we are and are expected to qualify.' Even the normally laid back and confident Browny was not quite as beaming as usual, but then she had just had a tooth accidentally knocked out by Jody Handley in training ahead of the game.

Come kick-off, though, and all that is forgotten. Williams settles nerves for the 12,164 strong crowd and her colleagues on the quarter hour with a powerful shot from a free-kick won by Eni Aluko thirty yards out, but keeper Sarah Bouhaddi is alive to the threat and keeps the ball out. Sue Smith watches from the bench as Rachel Yankey tests the France defence just before the half-hour mark with a free-kick that is almost nodded in by Karen Carney, who seems to have found a taste for headers after her goal against Iceland, but the youngster is off target. Moments later, it is Rachel Brown's goal that is under threat, the keeper dashing out to claim the ball ahead of a fiercely determined Laëtitia Tonazzi. Before France know it, England are on the attack again, Aluko cleverly cutting back to tee herself up for a near-post shot, but it is an easy catch for the keeper. The action swings back and Hoda Lattaf threatens before the break with a left-footed volley just past the far post. It is 0-0 but both sides have enjoyed chances and at half-time Powell pleads with her team to have a little more self-belief. 'I actually said to the girls, please don't tell me this side are better than you,' admits Powell later.

England need all they can muster when the second half sees Marinette Pichon, architect of England's play-off loss at Selhurst Park and a former Philadelphia Charge teammate of Kelly Smith's, shrug off illness to enter the attack. A minute later, the substitute heads what looks like a certain goal but Brown makes a vital fingertip save onto her left-hand post. 'It was like David Seaman in the FA Cup against Sheffield United,' says Williams, recalling the Arsenal keeper's flying leap to deny Paul Peschisolido in the 2003 FA Cup semi-finals. Brown clatters her head making the save and assumes everyone has missed her heroics until the physiotherapist and doctor say, 'Great save'. 'I thought no-one had seen and thought it was just Browny being stupid again,' she recalls. Brown has only just shaken that knock off when Tonazzi once again bears down on goal, forcing the keeper to palm a fine shot away from the net and the advancing Pichon. Two minutes later Casey Stoney, winning her thirty-seventh cap, hits a cross that dips late but over the bar. An exhausting final few minutes see the ball ping from end to end. Sonia Bompastor lays the ball back to Pichon on the edge of the area, but her snap shot is gathered by Brown. Williams volleys a last-gasp throw-in from Unitt over the bar and Pichon glides past Katie Chapman but loses out to Brown before she can lob the keeper. It is a nail-biting climax to a crunch match that leaves the campaign wide open.

'It was an exciting game for a goalie,' says Brown. 'The whole team battled, although in retrospect we gave them too much respect.' Too much respect or not, the point keeps England top of the table and very much in contention for that qualification spot. 'It's still four games to go. We can't discount Holland. They've got everything to play for so it's still open,' says Powell afterwards. As for Brown, Powell was not sure how well it reflected on her team for her goalkeeper to be named Player of the Match:

> At key moments she stood up, did well, kept us in it but equally I've got to praise everybody for their work rate, their effort… It was a hard game, it's been a long week, physically demanding and they all stepped up to the mark which is what we wanted so I can't ask for more than that.

But with four more games to play, Powell would ask for more. The question was, could her team live up to her demands?

Talk of the Town

A month on and England were back where they had started the campaign, facing Austria. The edgy draw against bitter rivals France meant England had the breathing space of a point over second-placed Holland, while whipping girls Austria had picked up a miserly one win in four matches since they met England in the opener back in September. Austria was still set to be a tough call, though, given that the England players were coming to the game off the back of a gruelling domestic season. A week previously, triumphant Arsenal had secured their place in the next season's UEFA Cup after lifting their third League title on the trot with a stylish 2-0 home victory over Charlton. But while England's Arsenal contingent were still buoyed by their success, it was a disappointing finish for Charlton players Katie Chapman, Eni Aluko and their skipper Casey Stoney. The trio had beaten Arsenal to the League Cup the previous month, but the coveted League title was the one prize Charlton had yet to collect under no-nonsense manager Keith Boanas. The Addicks were now left with a battle for pride and second place with the team that supplied much of the rest of the England team – Everton. Putting domestic woes aside as Austria approached and the international scene took precedence would be easier for mum-of-one Chapman than law student Aluko or Loughborough graduate Stoney.

A nasty gash on her foot ruled accomplished defender Stoney out, while Aluko was letting football play second fiddle to her career. The nineteen-year-old was in the throes of her first-year law exams at Brunel University in London and would reluctantly sit this one out. There were no such complications holding Addicks' midfielder Chapman back. The calf injury that had kept her out of just one of England's qualifiers thus far had healed and she was looking forward to bagging a forty-eighth cap for England in front of a few more familiar faces than usual. Playing at Gillingham in Kent meant this was virtually a home fixture for the Sidcup-based player and a good thirty or so family and friends, including several of the lads from her partner Mark's Saturday league team, Drummond Athletic, planned to cheer England on at Priestfield. Chapman's problem-free selection did not mean the player could not empathise with her teammates: missing out was an experience the young mum knew all about. A broken bone knitted together with a plate and two screws had kept Chapman out of Charlton's long-awaited FA Cup final triumph in May 2005. And when she was pregnant with son Harvey two seasons previously, Chapman had watched from the stands as England made a last desperate push to reach the World Cup 2003 and her club side Fulham played for treble silverware glory.

Chapman may have been absent from competitive action during those periods, but the blonde-haired darling of professional women's football was an ever-present in training. Battling beyond the pain inside her padded 'big white hand' to run out on the practice pitch with England had ensured Chapman stayed fit enough to make it to Euro 2005. While her desperation to play a part in Fulham's season had meant the midfielder was just as dogged about her training regime when she was carrying her child. For almost every day of her pregnancy, Chapman would pack her kit bag, clamber into the car, delicately strap a seat belt across her growing bump and drive across London to Fulham's training ground. She recalls:

> I carried on training, was in every day... I played up to eleven weeks and after that I carried on joining in with the girls. I could still do the shooting, skills and stuff like that and I think from about six months I went into the gym. I wanted to be back for the FA Cup final.

Harvey's birth by caesarean section put the kibosh on that plan: Fulham faced London rivals Charlton in the final scarcely a month later and Chapman would not be risked. But just as she had been earlier that season when Fulham secured the League and League Cup titles, Chapman was there to cheer her colleagues on. Casting a watchful eye over her toddler son as he plays amid a pile of toys in the front room of their neat home, Chapman insists she still revelled in the spectacle. 'I was so happy for the girls that they'd actually had a great season and they'd strived for everything they wanted and got it,' she says. 'I probably enjoyed it as much as they did, although I did want to play badly.'

That burning desire to be at the heart of the action first surfaced at primary school in Bermondsey when the sporty Chapman and her twin sister Sophie watched the lads passing a ball around in the playground. The urge to join in had more to do with not wanting to kick her heels during break time than any desperation to kick a ball, but it led to much more than that. 'I just took to it,' she says. 'Just because it was the main sport in the playground, you know, when you don't really want to stand around.' Millwall in the Community's women's and girls' football development officer Lou Waller turned those fun-filled playground kickabouts into something more purposeful. In 1992, Waller spotted the Chapman sisters' potential and recruited the ten-year-olds for the club that had boasted Hope Powell among its ranks. Given that the Chapmans were Millwall FC supporters, Lionesses' midfielder and England full-back Waller did not exactly have to sell the women's club to the sisters. She would have been on solid ground if she had, though. Set up in 1971, Millwall Lionesses had a proud history in the game. They were the first to affiliate to a professional men's club and start a centre of excellence and in the intervening years their various youth squads had become schools for success. 'It was pretty well run,' says Chapman. 'I think they were one of the better clubs at that time.'

The youngster became one of the better players too and within four years she was debuting for Millwall against Southampton Saints in the National Division. Shy off the pitch, Chapman is feisty on it and the slender teenager's winning mentality and athleticism ensured her presence in every game that season. Come May, Chapman set her reserve aside to join in as the Lionesses lustily roared, 'No one likes us, we don't care' while dancing deliriously with the FA Cup, League Cup and Mary Phillip's toddler son Jordan in their arms. Lou Waller's header had seen Millwall edge a tight 1-0 FA Cup victory over Wembley in front of 3,000 enthralled supporters at Upton Park. The Lionesses had also beaten Everton 2-1 at Barnet's Underhill ground to lift the League Cup. It was the end of a six-year major trophy drought for Millwall and the start of a silverware-rich career for Chapman. 'I was fourteen and we won both trophies and it's something special that I'll never forget,' she says. 'Millwall was one of the bigger clubs and the progression through the club was amazing, we had a great squad.' Her sister Sophie, Justine Lorton and Pauline Cope were teammates at that time. As was Chapman's future England colleague Mary Phillip. 'It was a great atmosphere,' Phillip recalls. 'Everyone was looking after each other and if one player got kicked, all of us felt it and you knew that your back was covered regardless.' As time went on, Chapman was not able to watch her sister's back. Sophie drifted away from the game before teaming up with Fulham then going on to enjoy life on a football scholarship at university in America. But the less well known, yet technically as talented twin switched off from the game for a while. Her sister, however, started to make waves in the England squad two years after her double-winning season.

Katie Chapman actually got the chance to dip her toe in the international waters during Millwall's triumphant term. 'Kate was probably the youngest ever player to be invited to the senior England set-up,' her then manager Jim Hicks recalls. But the call was felt to be a little too early for the fourteen-year-old and she declined the offer. Chapman admits:

> I was a bit too young... I was just into my first season and I was finding my feet and settling down and I was so surprised that I got called in, but

> I thought I needed a little bit more time to mature and get used to it, it was in too deep.

Once she took the plunge, Chapman's rise through the England ranks was as sure as her well-timed tackles. Caps for the newly formed Under-18s were the first step aged sixteen. Scoring in her fourth appearance, against Finland at Kettering Town, saw Chapman solidify her place in the England team that took on Norway in the quarter-finals of the Under-18 European Championship 1999. The young team, which also featured Casey Stoney, Amanda Barr, Rachel Brown and Rachel Unitt, lost 4-1 on aggregate. It was good experience, though, in a formative year in which the teenager impressed enough domestically to win the first ever FA Young Player of the Year award. Chapman's coolness under pressure as captain of the Under-18s the following season saw Powell call her in for England's Euro 2001 qualifier against Switzerland at Bristol, a month short of her eighteenth birthday. The Lioness fitted in at centre half for the final twenty minutes as Sue Smith's goal saw England through. Defence was not Chapman's favourite position, running the midfield and being 'the centre of everything' is her ideal. But Powell was keen to freshen up the England back line, so defence it would have to be. Chapman did not care. 'I would have played anywhere, even in goal,' she laughs. England's new recruit would not need to don a green jersey to stay in the side, however. When Norway hosted England less than a month later in Moss, near Oslo, Chapman was handed the no.3 shirt and asked to line up alongside captain Mo Marley from the first whistle. It was the kind of start that could have had a fledgling international fearing her career was over before it had begun. Norway inflicted the visitors' heaviest ever defeat when they battered England a whopping 8-0. It did not affect Chapman's chances one iota. 'Once I started I pretty much stayed,' she says. Why? Powell recognised that Chapman possessed a sound technique, physical toughness and a crucial devotion to fitness at a time when the most that was expected of players was twice-weekly training after work.

Powell knew before she had even taken charge of the England set-up that something had to give in that department:

> I saw that we were losing games in the last ten minutes and so basically had to change the culture from training twice a week with your club to training five days a week… They can play football, but if you're too knackered in a game to compete against the Germans you're not going to shine, even if you're Kelly Smith, you won't shine if you can't last ninety minutes.

Demonstrating that improved fitness could bring success were Fulham's professionals. With the luxury of funding from chairman Mohamed Al Fayed, they were out on the training pitch five days a week. Within three years they had swept aside every team in the women's game. The improvements in those players' fitness levels did not go unnoticed by Powell as she told women's football magazine *She Kicks* in 2001:

> You just have to look at the likes of Katie Chapman who for me is the best young player in the country… She has played for the 18s, the seniors and in the cup final she covered every blade of grass. If we had eleven players of that level of fitness it would help me and it can only help the clubs as well.

Daily training was a change in tack for those England players not under professional contracts, though. 'Four years ago pretty much none of us did that,' says goalkeeper Rachel Brown. 'It's a simple matter of fact, it wasn't expected of us. Now it's thoroughly expected.' Weight training, speed work, recovery sessions, endurance training: they are all part of the programme that England expects of its players today, despite their amateur status. 'It's hard doing a weight programme when you've been working all day, you have to be motivated, especially in the cold weather,' says Fara Williams. But with personal trainers helping the England elite along and regional testing monitoring the fruits of their efforts, the sessions cannot be ducked. 'Before you could maybe just go on a Sunday and get away with playing and being good,' says Alex Scott, who supplements her training with daily runs. 'But now, if you're not putting in the training, you do get found out.'

A wish not just to be good but to 'be one of the best' has meant Chapman's coaches at every level have witnessed her commitment to training. As a semi-professional with Charlton from 2004 to 2006 and then with Arsenal, Chapman would urge her partner Mark to strap their son into the child seat on his bike so she could pound the pavements with them riding alongside like trainers preparing a boxer for the fight of her life. Her attitude was equally as rigorous when still an amateur. 'In those days at Millwall, the fitness and training was brilliant,' she says. 'When I was young I couldn't stay still so I did a lot of stuff.' The training bar was raised when Chapman brought eight years with Millwall to a close to join Fulham shortly after her England debut in 2000. Fulham's was a regime that saw players train on Monday, twice on a Tuesday and Thursday, once again on a Friday, light training and set pieces on a Saturday ready for a match on the Sunday. Her manager in her early Fulham years, Frank McMorrow, remembers the player giving her all to every session. 'Katie trains like she plays, takes no prisoners and she's a tremendous role model for anyone who wants to train well,' he says. 'She's 100 per cent committed and will go through brick walls to train.' So rather than baulk at the thought of turning out in all weathers day in, day out, Chapman relished the extra graft professional status offered. 'I absolutely loved it,' she says. 'I loved going in every day, doing that work because it was something I wanted to do. Every player that has been at Fulham felt the same and if I could go back to then, I would.'

By the time Harvey was born in April 2003, those heady days of professionalism were coming to an end. It had been a fruitful time for Chapman who notched up a second FA Young Player of the Year award; three slots in Euro 2001 where she was officially recognised for her technical ability by watching coaches; a well-taken

Even a broken hand cannot keep Katie Chapman (centre) away from training for long.

goal in front of 2.5 million viewers in the first BBC1 televised FA Cup final victory of 2002 against Donny Belles; and an International Player of the Year gong. She was still only twenty years old. 'It was like I was on a high getting all these things,' she says. 'I was shocked.' Chapman's girl-next-door looks did not go unnoticed either and the player dubbed by the *Evening Standard* as 'the finest of England's rich batch of teenage talent' posed as a cover girl in *She Kicks* magazine, standing shoulder to shoulder with future England men's team players Michael Carrick and Joe Cole, and joined 'Goldenballs' David Beckham at the NEC in Birmingham to parade the first England women's kit.

But it was not her golden-girl image that had club and country clamouring for Chapman's return once she and Mark had their bouncing baby boy in their arms. Come the start of 2003/04 Fulham's semi-professionals were embarking on their first UEFA Cup campaign, while England were preparing for Euro 2005 with a string of friendlies. Five months and a day since Harvey's birth, Chapman returned to Hope Powell's line-up in the midfield lynchpin role she had graduated to in the aftermath of Euro 2001. That narrow 1-0 win as England took on Australia's Matildas for the first time ever was far from a waltz in the park, but there were no heavy legs on Player of the Match Chapman's part. Any post-pregnancy cobwebs had already been blown off in Fulham's 1-0 Community Shield victory over Doncaster Belles and their first group-stage UEFA Cup matches. Chapman's two goals against Faroe Islands champions KÍ Klaksvik and another brace against Moldova's leading club FC Codru Anenii Noi helped Fulham rise to the top of Group Eight to book a quarter-final spot with former UEFA Cup champions Frankfurt. It was an upbeat start to life as semi-professionals, but Chapman admits she found matters much changed. The Scandinavian internationals that had bolstered the prize-winning side had gone and, as football was no longer a paying job, training had reverted to the evenings so players could make their living by day.

> Now, you were going out of a night and getting back late, which I was used to before I went there, but having those three years had changed the whole concept of it... We were at the training ground then, Motspur Park, and we had the use of the gym. I'd get down there early and go and do some work in the gym, do a run and stuff and then I'd go out and play the football later. So I just kept myself fit that way.

Chapman's fitness would be sorely tested in the coming season as Fulham faced Birgit Prinz's immense Frankfurt side in the UEFA Cup and battled to retain the three domestic trophies they had won the previous season. But Fulham ended the term with just the Community Shield to their name and Chapman would hook up with London rivals Charlton that summer. 'We didn't win much but it wasn't a bad season,' she shrugs. 'I think you get to a point sometimes when you just think you've had enough, you need something different, a new challenge and that's what happened unfortunately.'

It was an urge that her new club-mate, the striker Eniola Aluko, had felt when she left Birmingham in January 2004 to sign for Charlton under former Tooting and Mitcham men's team manager Keith Boanas. The Blues had put Aluko on the road to England recognition, nurturing the speedy striker since the day the tiny twelve-year-old signed from Leafield Athletic. Nigerian-born Aluko was only six months old when her politician father Daniel and his wife Sheila moved to England and the Birmingham suburb of Kings Norton. She soon stumbled upon the game on the streets around her home alongside younger brother Sone. A law student in the making, Aluko would dash home from the street games in time to watch her favourite television programmes such as *The Bill*. But not before she had matched younger brother Sone goal for goal. 'It was something to look forward to,' she recalls. 'And obviously the more you play the better you get at it and I got really quite good. I think some of the best players in the world will say they learnt their trade on the streets and that's how I started playing football.' Sone Aluko got good too and was picked up by Birmingham FC's academy while his sister led the front line for teams at Broadmeadow Primary School and Leafield Athletic.

Across the city, professional footballer Marcus Bignot had taken to rushing home from training with Crewe Alexandra to assume his duties in charge of Birmingham's women's team. The ambitious manager was assembling a squad of talented Midlanders in a bid to reach the holy grail of the National Division and once he heard of Aluko's potential he was keen to add her to his roster. Visiting her parents at home, the enthusiastic professional set out his plans. 'I told them how we invest in youth, how we coach them,' recalls Bignot. Aluko repaid her manager's faith in her by the time she was just fifteen, Birmingham benefiting from their striker's killer pace and eye for goal as they marched towards promotion to the National Division and a League Cup final date with Katie Chapman's Fulham. Promotion was delivered, but the professionals stamped on the Blues' cup-winning dreams, seeing off the team dubbed 'Bignot's Babes' by an emphatic seven goals to one in the final. Chapman headed home the first and last of those goals. But for a team with an average age of eighteen, even reaching the final was a feat. 'It showed the quality we had throughout our team in terms of youth and credit to Marcus Bignot to be honest because he really instilled a quality in us that was great,' says Aluko. 'If you look at a lot of the players who played in that final now, half of them are in the senior team.'

Just over four years after signing on the dotted line for Birmingham, the level-headed Aluko had her eye on a different senior team – England's. With a Young Player of the Year award and call-ups for the Under-17s and 19s in her locker by the end of 2003, Aluko made the first of many pragmatic career decisions and opted to leave her home-town club. 'I think you get to a point in life where you need another challenge,' she says. 'You need to challenge yourself more, see what more you can do for yourself and I was at that point at Birmingham.' It was a transfer that had surprised many in the game. But like Karen Carney when she eventually left the Blues, it was one Aluko had mulled over for months. 'It was quite a big build-up but I wouldn't have made a quick decision anyway, Birmingham is a club I love and I grew up with,' she says. 'Obviously it was upsetting, but Charlton was one of the most established women's teams in the country, if not the most established team in the country, so it was something I was looking forward to.'

Since they were formed in 2000, when Charlton men took the FA Cup and League champions Croydon as their women's team, the Addicks have consistently held their own in the top flight. The semi-professionals enjoy strong backing from their men's club and boast youth sides, a centre of excellence and an academy. Aluko was joining an ambitious Addicks side that was chasing silverware on three fronts, but beating Chapman's Fulham 1-0 in the final of the League Cup secured their only pot that year. By the summer of 2005, however, the speedy striker was joining old adversary Chapman on Charlton's winners' podium after her solo goal against Everton from a neat pass by Emma Coss had finally secured the FA Cup trophy for the

Eniola Aluko relishes the challenge of leading the line for Charlton.

Addicks on the third time of asking. Chapman's broken hand, picked up on England duty against Scotland, ruled her out of what would have been automatic selection in the Charlton line-up. But she still joined Aluko and Co. to celebrate in front of 8,567 fans at Upton Park while old pal and Everton defender Rachel Unitt tugged up her Toffees' shirt to flash a 'get well' message on her vest.

Their season, along with their ecstatic skipper Casey Stoney's, would be extended that year as they were named in Hope Powell's Euro 2005 squad. Aluko had starred for the Under-19s in the European Championship in Germany two years previously, but since making her senior debut in England's 2-1 win over Holland in September 2004, she had only made eight appearances for England's seniors ahead of the tournament. Yet if scoring the FA Cup-winning goal for Charlton had propelled Aluko into the nation's consciousness as a peak audience of 1.4 million tuned into the final on the BBC that May, the Euros would make the pacey forward a household name. As it turned out, Aluko was unable to add to the first

Charlton captain Casey Stoney holds aloft the FA Cup in 2005, won by a single goal from Eniola Aluko (11, centre).

senior goal she had recorded against the Czech Republic ten days before the Euros kicked off. But her electric runs and plucky schoolgirl story garnered her plenty of attention that summer.

The articulate 'Babs' as Aluko has been dubbed by Chelsea fan Fara Williams in honour of Nigerian defender Celestine Babayaro, was one of England's students and the Euros fell smack in the middle of the eighteen-year-old's A-level exams. The tale of Aluko sitting a history exam on the day she was due to line up against Denmark at Ewood Park made great headlines for the papers. It was not such great news for a youngster who found the whole England experience as demanding as her studies. 'It's a very intense environment,' she says. 'There's rest and recovery, you have to keep drinking, you have to keep hydrated, you have to ensure your performance is good, you have to analyse with the team – it's very intense, it feels like doing a degree at times.' The demands on Aluko were even more rigorous given that only a first-rate performance in her exams would land a place on her real degree course.

That course was law, a subject that had fascinated Aluko since she turned on the television as a primary school pupil to watch police procedurals like *The Bill*. 'I had this infatuation with the police when I was younger,' Aluko admits. Sheila Aluko says it was a love that almost led her daughter into a career with the force, until she convinced her otherwise. Sheila says:

> When she was young she had this thing about law and order... She would not miss *The Bill*, at about five or six, she loved it and would analyse it and was fascinated with it. She wanted to join the police but I told her I think you'll be too small – all I could think about were riots.

Yet her desire to make it on to Brunel University's law course was not just to fulfil a childhood fantasy. It was also an insurance policy should the chance to pursue a career as a professional footballer not materialise:

> If you're paying subs to play football or if you're spending more to play football then you have to kind of say, hold on a minute, I need to invest in my future in terms of education so I will earn... I come from a family that see education as extremely important and the state of women's football now, there's not the financial security that you'd like or that the men get so you have to put your energy into other things that might give financial benefits in the future.

Which explained why Aluko would set England aside during the campaign in order to prepare for her exams. 'It was something I had to do, I had to take my exams,' she says. 'It's not nice, you always want to play for your country but university can't make an exception for me.'

Aluko's predicament would force her out of both this match against Austria and the date with Hungary the following month. But this was a player Hope Powell could not ignore. The hangover from the senior and Under-19 Euros, which her manager Keith Boanas

Left and below: After Charlton beat Arsenal in the League Cup final 2006, Katie Chapman celebrates with son Harvey while Player of the Match Eniola Aluko shows off the trophy itself.

says, 'left her tired for a long time', had been cured as the season progressed. So much so that when the final whistle blew in the League Cup final on 5 March 2006 Eni Aluko was the talk of the town. Two weeks after her nineteenth birthday, the tiny striker had outfoxed Arsenal's defence to score two glorious goals at a Wycombe Wanderers ground enlivened by a record League Cup crowd totalling 3,506 supporters. It was the kind of form that showed why Powell had persisted in playing Aluko throughout the qualification campaign and one that ensured she would be recalled by the time Holland came calling at Charlton FC's Valley ground in August.

But on 20 April 2006, Aluko had her head in her books as England walked out at Priestfield to the cheers of 8,068 expectant fans ready to be entertained by the home nation's finest. Coming in for the injured Casey Stoney, Everton's Lindsay Johnson gets her second start of the campaign and slots in at right-back, while taking Aluko's spot is her former Charlton colleague, the goal-hungry Amanda Barr. Despite Austria's attempts to throw a wall of steel around Kelly Smith, she still manages to thread a pass to Barr, but defender Susanne Just is having none of it. It is a slow start but the Chapman entourage are on their feet twenty minutes in as the midfielder shapes to shoot only to volley over. 'It was frustrating but I think we knew it was going to come, we just needed to settle ourselves,' recalls Chapman. Smith continues to find space, unleashing a turn and shot that flies wide and Rachel Yankey is in with a chance but side-foots Barr's cross straight at Bianca Reischer. England's pressure pays off, though, as Yankey's corner is unwittingly turned into Austria's net by despairing skipper Sonja Spieler. Fara Williams looks to increase England's tally when she turns on the style just before the break. But the midfielder's show of close control is not matched by her finishing and she misses the target. England stride into the changing room a goal to the good but it should be much more.

Things are not going England's way after the restart. Karen Carney sees a goal disallowed for handball and there is a moment of worry for the Chapman clan as their player is felled by a clash of heads.

But the hardy mum shrugs off the collision and England rally with Williams powering in a point-blank header that is heroically blocked by Reischer. The crowd urge England on but as the final five minutes approach, there is still only one goal in it and as Austria have their tails up, there is every chance England could blow it. 'It was starting to look like, oh God, they are going to score and it's going to be 1-1, that kind of feeling,' admits Powell afterwards. But the manager throws on Sue Smith for Yankey and the game is turned on its head. Moments later, Williams puts the ball in the back of the net from a cut-back by Kelly Smith on the right after the Arsenal star skips past three defenders on the byline. Two minutes later Sue Smith drifts into the box and plants her head firmly onto Lindsay Johnson's inch-perfect cross, wheeling away in delight as the ball pings into the bottom right-hand corner. 'I could see it coming over and everyone was laughing at my technique because I did it all textbook,' Smith recalls afterwards. Victory was in the bag, but there is more to come and in the dying seconds, fifty-ninth-minute substitute Jody Handley punishes Spieler's weak headed back pass by steering the ball past the onrushing Bianca Reischer.

England have made heavy weather of it for sure, but Powell is content with her two super subs, three goals in eight minutes and three more points in the bag. 'It's the end of our season and there are tired legs perhaps, not that that's an excuse,' she says. 'The most important thing is four goals, three points, I'm happy with that.'

Given the Chance

Three games to go and England were now being pursued by rivals France who had overtaken Holland and were lying three points off the top spot. England's upcoming opponents in mid-May, Hungary, had had the stuffing knocked out of them in the away tie back in October 2005. That 13-0 win had been the biggest rampage in England's first unbeaten season since the days of Ted Copeland twelve years earlier. Powell's confident side did not expect their visitors to roll over quite so easily this time, but victory at Southampton's St Mary's Stadium was a must. It was one that would have to be achieved without first-choice picks Eni Aluko, Kelly Smith, Fara Williams or Katie Chapman, however. Williams had amassed two yellow cards so would join the rested Chapman to watch from the stands. While law student Aluko, who had an exam looming, and her rested England colleague Smith would offer their insights into the match to BBC3 viewers. They would have plenty to talk about as Hungary attempted to test the strength of Powell's bench. Coming off it to fill the gaps in the starting XI that night were old England room-mates Vicky Exley and Sue Smith, Everton striker Jody Handley and Loughborough scholar Jo Potter, a tricky winger who had hit the back of the net in the record-breaking 13-goal Hungary victory. Taking a place on the substitutes' bench for only the first time was Arsenal's hotly tipped teenage striker Lianne Sanderson. Next to her was fellow Gunner Alex Scott, who was hoping to resume her position as Powell's first-choice right-back following a knee injury. As it turned out, the entire group would play their part as England sought a second dismissal of defence-minded Hungary. But it was Exley and Scott, players at either end of the England spectrum of age and experience, who would deal the killer blows.

Getting your own hotel room while playing away with England is no mean feat, but it is one Vicky Exley has achieved. If she did not, the unfortunate player picked to room with her would probably wake up in the middle of the night with 'Tricky', as she is known, noisily trying to bed down in the hotel wardrobe. 'We'd find her in the cupboards or in the bath,' laughs ex-roomie Sue Smith. 'A few times I've woken up and she's over me, shouting.' Exley good-naturedly denies it all. If you bring the subject up, she cries:

> You know I haven't done it for ages! Mind you, I don't share with anyone at the moment; they won't let me because they say I keep everyone awake. I've always done it. As a child I'd end up in my mum's bedroom and she'd go, 'Back to sleep!' I'd be in the airing cupboard or looking out the window. Everyone says, you should go to these clinics and see what's in your brain, see what's going on and I'm like, no!

Anyone who has ever followed Exley's lengthy career knows exactly what kind of brain the Doncaster Belles stalwart possesses – a footballer's. How else do you explain more than a decade in the top flight, almost half a century of England caps, Player of the Month plaudits, international goals and an England captaincy?

The Donny Belle was first handed an England cap against Italy way back in 1996 when she raced on to the field in the southern city of Cosenza for the last twenty minutes of a European qualifier that the visitors lost 2-1. The doughty midfielder made more of an impact in her second appearance, replacing an injured Hope Powell twenty minutes into the game this time and going on to bag a goal alongside Kelly Smith in a 2-0 win over Croatia in Osijek. 'Hope got injured after, like, twenty minutes, and I went on and scored,' she says. 'I can remember it, a cross and a right-foot shot into the corner of the net.'

Exley was twenty at the time and had only been playing competitive football for a handful of years, formerly with Sheffield Wednesday in the old Division One North and latterly with Doncaster Belles in the National Division.

It had been a worthwhile move across Yorkshire for the Rotherham-born player. The Belles had a rich trophy-winning tradition and were six-times FA Cup winners by the time Exley signed up for Paul Edmunds' side at the start of the 1994/95 season. Walking into the lively Donny changing rooms at Stainforth for the first time that summer, eighteen-year-old Exley knew she had joined a club that would be a lot of fun to play for. 'It was brilliant,' Exley smirks. 'It was probably one of the best years because of the team spirit and the players just used to stick together, if one did something, we'd all; there would be no little groups.' The working-class Yorkshire lasses that made up the Belles of the 1990s needed a first-rate team spirit – they had a lot to live up to. Formed as Belle Vue Ladies in 1969 by, as legend has it, women selling raffle tickets in the stands at Doncaster Rovers men's ground, they had become Doncaster Belles by 1971 and were founder members of the National League twenty years later. They laid waste to the league that historic season, finishing unbeaten and securing the FA Cup and League double. Exley arrived just as the Belles were about to enter a trophy drought, however. No major silverware had been won since the Belles claimed the FA Cup and League titles in 1994, but it was not for the want of trying. The Belles had come close to winning the league six times, finishing as runners-up on all half-dozen occasions, and they reached two prestigious FA Cup finals, but had to look on as their opponents raised high the trophy that was their club's for so many years. Throughout it all, 'Tricky' had been a guiding force, scoring against Croydon as Belles lost 2-1 in the FA Cup 2000 and, two years later, battling against Fulham's professionals only to lose by the same scoreline at Crystal Palace in front of the first live BBC1 FA Women's Cup audience.

In the intervening years, Exley has gone from being one of the giggling girls in a team filled with larger-than-life characters, made famous in Pete Davies' book *I Lost My Heart to the Belles*, to the Yorkshire side's saviour. The reason a team like Belles needed a saviour? Come the summer of 2004, the club had witnessed an exodus of key players. England stalwart Karen Walker and twins Gemma and Carly Hunt left to join former manager Julie Chipchase at rivals Leeds and Jody Handley and Becky Easton had opted for the blue shirts of Everton. In short, a string of first-teamers moved on to pastures new, apart from the club's veterans Mandy 'Flo' Lowe, Claire 'Dezzie' Utley and their teammate, down-to-earth postwoman Vicky 'Tricky' Exley. 'I think no-one really knew what they wanted to do and then I think two people left, and then two more thought I might leave and everyone was thinking, "Oh well, two more have left, I'm going to go",' she shrugs. 'It was a bit like that really. We were left with a lot of young kids.' A lot of youngsters there may have been, but they were ones who looked up to the then twenty-eight-year-old England veteran – after all, she had coached several of them since they were ten-years-old and she was not about to let them down.

The Belles had never finished lower than fifth in their entire tenure in the National Division. But in 18 miserable games that term, they only managed to put the ball into their opponents' nets 10 times. Three wins were mustered and it was a nail-biting finish to the season with four teams mired in the relegation dogfight. Fittingly, it was skipper Exley who pulled the Belles back from the brink, heading in a sixty-eighth-minute goal against Birmingham City on the last day of the season to stave off relegation by the slimmest of margins – two points. 'If she hadn't stayed at the Belles, the Belles would have went under because she's kind of carried them,' says their manager, Scotsman John Buckley. 'She's been brilliant in the sense that she's not just a good club captain but she's carried a lot of young ones on her back.' Exley's role in the Belles' fightback won her a bottle of Player of the Month champagne that April. It was double reward for a loyalty born out of the belief that the good times could one day return. Exley says:

> Well, we've always had a good team, haven't we?I thought, I'm going to stay, try and keep the team together because I didn't want them to go down and you know, people did come in to try and sign me but I just weren't interested in leaving. I did think about it and then just decided it would be better to stay at Belles and hopefully we'll build and we did really, we built again.

A fourth-placed finish in the league the following season signalled a beefed-up Belles' revival and by 2007, some more literal building work had given the club fresh impetus. Having linked with the men's team in the 2003/04 season, Doncaster Rovers Belles, as they became known, now ground-share the city's flash new 15,000 capacity Keepmoat community stadium with Doncaster Rovers FC, Lakers rugby team and Doncaster Athletics Club. That agreement guarantees the women's club six games on the main pitch a season and six more on the sister pitch next door, coupled with office space, state-of-the-art changing rooms and use of the restaurant. It is the kind of home ground most female footballers can only dream of. An FA and Football Foundation survey in 2003 looked at 45,000 pitches and found ninety-four per cent did not have changing facilities for women players, something the two bodies say they hope to improve with a cash injection of £20 million into community facilities. But it was not just having decent changing rooms and toilets that gave Donny a boost. Having a state-of-the-art ground to call their own meant the club's opening match at Keepmoat, an all-Yorkshire derby day tie against Leeds, was watched by 1,797 fans. It was the kind of attendance that could make women's football self-supporting if it was achieved by every club week in, week out. It was also one that on that particular January day lifted the teams with the kind of electric atmosphere only usually found at cup finals. It was a proud and promising moment for their skipper. 'We've got the facilities,' says Exley. 'We've got the players, we just need to keep working.'

The same bullish enthusiasm that got Exley through the Belles' dark days has served the player throughout her life. Unable to compete for her school team because of mixed-football age-group rules,

Belles' captain Vicky Exley battles through the mud in a league game against Chelsea.

the young Yorkshire lass simply trained with the boys anyway. 'I wasn't allowed to play because of the age group where you're not allowed to,' she says. 'But I always trained and used to score loads of goals past all the lads. I can remember that.' It was a make-do-and-mend situation in an era when girls' leagues were few and far between and many players dropped by the wayside. But Exley loved the game and as soon as she was old enough to score goals in a women's league, she signed for Sheffield Wednesday. Battling every weekend on muddy pitches in the gritty Division One North, as it was then known, suited the teenager. But after a while the increasingly skilful and speedy player set her sights on the Premier League and England. When Donny came in for Exley a few months short of her nineteenth birthday, she was ready to move. 'I made my mind up in a week,' she says. 'Like, I want to play in the Premier League, I want to get noticed, my ambition was always to play for England so that's what I did.'

By the time Euro 2001 came around, Hope Powell had named five Donny Belles in her squad of twenty to represent England in Germany. Postwoman Exley had played a somewhat meagre 16 times in five years by the eve of that competition, but she would not be coming home from her rounds to watch highlights of her contemporaries in action on the telly. Exley had been included in the squad and would swap her postwoman uniform for the designer trouser suits and sunglasses that the team donned before they boarded the plane at Luton. Her post office work mates in Rotherham were almost as eager for her to play for England in Germany as she was. 'They were excited,' she recalls. 'Everyone was rooting for me and people were really interested in me playing, everyone said, "Show 'em what you can do".' The posties' colleague only got fifteen minutes of fame during those Euros, coming on for Sammy Britton against Germany in a 3-0 defeat. She would run the rule over England from the bench again come the next European Championship. A good 25 more caps had been racked up by the time she replaced Kelly Smith at half-time against Denmark in Euro 2005. The most recent of those caps included one in which she skippered the side to victory over Holland, getting on the scoresheet in the process, while others came at the Algarve Cup where she netted a brace. But in the Euros, Exley only got forty-five minutes to impress as England fared little better on home soil than they had in Germany in 2001. Regardless of the outcome, the support the home nation received in the north-west that summer of 2005 still brought a lump to the veteran's throat. 'When we got to Man City and it was like 30,000 people there watching,' says Exley. 'And when we pulled up with the coach and they were cheering "Come On England", it was a memory that you'd just never forget.'

Appreciative crowds were not restricted to the north-west that summer – they were at it in east London too. At least they were in Alex Scott's street. Driving into the street in Poplar where she shares a terraced house with her mum Carol and brother Ronnie, the bubbly England right-back was met by applause and posters of her-

Vicky Exley gives the fans something to remember at Ewood Park.

self in her neighbours' windows. 'Everyone was out clapping, I was just like, oh,' she says. 'And you had all the kids knocking on the door, didn't you?' adds her mum, looking on proudly in the cosy kitchen of their east London home. 'Yeah, they said, "Can I have your autograph Alex?" and I was like, you see me every day!' Little wonder 'Scottie' was slightly bemused by the reaction to her Euro 2005 displays. The Eastender played all 270 minutes of England's tournament. Yet her first call-up had arrived just nine months previously in the game that had seen the squad serenade Vicky Exley with the chant 'Tricky is our leader' as the Belle debuted as captain. Indeed, Scott had only actually picked up ten senior caps before her inclusion in the Euro squad and was still pinching herself to have been walking out with the England seniors at all. 'That year was just kind of mad for me,' she says. 'I just wanted to be playing week-in, week-out on a Sunday and I didn't even expect to be in the Euros for England.'

Everything is looking good for Alex Scott since she claimed her place in the England team.

Having coached Scott at Under-19 level, Mo Marley had a little more faith in her than the player possessed herself and had told her so a couple of years previously. 'She called me into a meeting and was like, "I see you as a future captain and you will make the senior side",' Scott recalls. Did she tell anyone? No. 'I think that's where my shyness comes in because I'm not someone to go and boast,' Scott shrugs. 'No, I kind of just kept it to myself.' The reason Marley had felt compelled to give that pep talk was in part down to Scott's fears over her fitful club appearances. Having come up through Arsenal's ranks since the age of eight, Scott had made the first team by seventeen. But as a striker in a team bursting with talented goal getters, including her best mate Ellen Maggs, England striker Angela Banks and Scotland skipper Julie Fleeting, she was still only a bit-part player. Former England captain Marley would include the East End-raised youngster in her plans anyway and Scott featured in two

Under-19 European finals and the World Cup in Canada. But the England youth-team coach was not the only one who was willing to make room for the robust youngster. Birmingham City manager Marcus Bignot took her away from Highbury the year before Euro 2005 with the promise of first-team action. Before too long, an England defender was born.

Rather than use Scott as a striker as Arsenal and England had, Bignot placed her in midfield as his thrusting new-look Birmingham City side sought to challenge the big guns for honours in 2005. When an injury to defender Faye Cardin ahead of a crucial league match against Everton forced Bignot to look for a replacement, he came up with Alex Scott. 'She has a tremendous work rate, not shy of a tackle and really is a ball winner,' says Bignot. 'We felt playing her in the middle of the park would develop her football but the long-term plan was always going to be as a full-back.' Scott was not so sure:

> I'll never forget. He just come into the changing room and he was like, 'Al, you'll think I've gone a bit mad but you're going to play right-back this game' and I was like, right-back? And he was like, 'Yeah yeah, just trust me'. He knew that I'd say yeah because I just wanted to play.

Bignot, a right-back himself, would only call on his midfielder to fill the gap at the back a couple more times that season. Hope Powell would go much further. The England boss was in the stands for Scott's defensive debut and the next thing the die-hard Arsenal fan knew, she was being asked to give it a go in a senior England shirt against Holland. 'It was all kind of a shock because that's the first time I'd ever even thought about playing right-back,' she shrugs. 'When I went to Holland I didn't even expect to play. I'd just been called up off stand-by because Kirsty Pealling had dropped out. I just went there for experience.' Not according to Powell. The England manager turned to Scott in the middle of her team talk in Heerhugowaard and told her she was coming on. 'I remember Brent [Hills] saying to me, "Don't look so scared",' Scott says. 'And I remember just going on and thinking I've got nothing to lose, I'm happy-go-lucky to be there and I did really well and just stayed there.'

It was that kind of give-it-a-go attitude that had landed the childhood tomboy her initial break into the world of women's football in the first place. Scott had torn her tights in break-time games at school and thrown herself into manic fifteen-a-side games against rival estates alongside brother Ronnie, a former Queens Park Rangers trialist. But after she was called on to make up the numbers in a neighbourhood competition when Ronnie's team was short of a player, her eagerness to play opened a new door. The referee was an Arsenal scout and within weeks, Scott was an Arsenal player.

Swapping the scrap of grass on her estate for Highbury's indoor stadium, Scott was thrown straight into the youth set-up where she teamed up with striker Ellen 'Maggsy' Maggs and the pair would relish coming up against Chelsea's Fara Williams and Eartha Pond in hotly contested matches. 'Arsenal was my life and it was like, get home from school, go and play at the ball court with Arsenal and it was kind of that's all I did,' Scott recalls. The youngster would take a break from Highbury occasionally, but only when she was asked to join England's Under-16s. Scott had been rejected in her first ever England try-out and she cried her heart out afterwards. 'You used to only have thirty minutes to try and prove in an eleven-a-side match what you can do, so it was hard,' she says. 'I remember getting that letter and crying and my mum putting her arm round me. At that age you think "I'm never going to play for England".' Mum Carol recalls reassuring her daughter saying, 'It'll come, one day it'll come.' And so it did, Scott rolling up to her first England camp in Telford with a suitcase almost as big as she was. 'I didn't know what to take,' she laughs. 'You just pack everything but you hardly need anything because everything's supplied for you. It was embarrassing.'

Scott felt just as self-conscious when news of her England call-up reached home and prompted a flurry of interest at her school Langdon Park. 'They used to say, "We want you to stand up in assembly" and I used to be like, no way,' Scott says. 'I didn't really see the bigger picture of it, other kids wanted to follow in your footsteps and I didn't really see that. Now I do.' Scott returned to school after the Euros to present a signed England shirt. Back then, though, the schoolgirl just wanted to play football, be it against visiting teams or Arsenal's reserves. 'We were straight in with the big ones and they were no messing, proper defenders,' she says. 'They'd kick you before they got the ball and me and Ellen used to be so small running around but we used to love it.' Arsenal did not just offer the effervescent player a football outlet, though. Signing up for their youth academy meant Scott could develop a career off the pitch by studying for a BTEC and practising coaching at summer schools. The teenager was making her way in the England Under-19s by this stage, but by 2004 had spent a second season on the fringes of Arsenal's first team and a move was inevitable. Experiencing the thrill of a World Cup in Canada with the Under-19s, where Scott, Fara Williams, Anita Asante and Co. had rubbed shoulders with US star Heather O'Reilly and Canada striker Christine Sinclair had fuelled her England ambition. If it burnt bright by the time she signed for Birmingham, it was red hot by the time she actually ran out with them. That summer, Scott was called into the first ever England Under-21 side that travelled to Iceland to play against the cream of Scandinavian youth football in the Nordic Cup. Two months later she had made her bow in the England seniors, impressing enough at right-back in the friendlies that followed to land the position for the Euros.

Signing for the team that threw her into the defensive spotlight turned out to be a shrewd move. But it was not without its complexities. There was the small matter of travelling from London to Birmingham for training and home matches for a start. To her surprise, Scott had an ally. Walking into the Blues' changing room, the new girl did a double take – former Arsenal teammate Ellen Maggs had followed her old pal to the Midlands without actually telling her. 'It was so weird, I was like, what are you doing here?' she recalls. Whenever possible, Maggs, fellow Londoner Rachel Yankey and Scott would motor up the M1 together to training. It was always preferable given the experience Scott had had when she attempted to catch the train. Queens Park Rangers player Bignot was running the team like a professional men's side and woe betide anyone who turned up late, which Scott did one day after a ticket mix-up meant she could only catch a later train. Bignot showed little mercy:

> I phoned Marcus and I was like, look Marcus, I'm going to be late... He was like, 'Well, you're going to get fined'. And I was like, but you're not paying me and I'm going to get fined my expenses? I can't come the following week then. He was like, 'So? It's properly run like this, this is a professional club.' I was so mad at him.

It was a strict regime, but one which would benefit Scott in the long run. As would joining up with Rachel Unitt and England's exercise scientist Dawn Scott at Lilleshall National Sports Centre on her days off in the lead up to the Euros and the Under-21s Nordic Cup.

Scott's weekly mileage would be vastly reduced by the time the two tournaments were over. Coming home from Nordic Cup action – having helped steer England to an impressive third place with three goals, one scored while skippering the side against Sweden while Sven-Göran Eriksson watched from the stands – Scott was ready for another season with Birmingham. But the club had lost its sponsorship and Scott would follow some of the other recent recruits who had moved on to pastures new. It was more pastures not so new where Scott was concerned, however. Vic Akers offered his old striker the chance to re-sign for Arsenal, this time as his first-choice right-back. But her return to the fold did not end there. Scott also went back to her BTEC days, not as a student but as a sports science lecturer to sixteen- to eighteen-year-old male rugby players and Arsenal academy girls. 'They're always asking for my shirts,' Scott laughs. 'So in my lessons I do quizzes and whoever wins the quiz, I give them a signed England shirt – it makes them learn at the same time.' To keep her students in prized England shirts, Scott would need to remain in pole position for the World Cup qualifiers.

Alex Scott has had to battle back from injury to retain her England spot.

And so it proved, initially at least, as Scott played an hour against Austria in the opening game and bagged her first senior goals for England with a brace in the 13-0 obliteration of Hungary. By the time England travelled to Holland in November, however, Scott was not making the journey with the team. She was lolling around in the back of Vic Akers' car with a gammy leg. A medial knee ligament injury, picked up ironically against Birmingham, had seen the player's right leg encased in plaster. Nonetheless, she was still desperate to watch England and so hitched a lift with Arsenal manager Akers and his assistant Fred Donnelly. Akers was used to travelling long distances to watch his players run out for England. The Arsenal men's kit manager was no stranger to making cross-Channel trips alongside the occasional player either, having accompanied his golf partner, Arsenal's flight-phobic striker Dennis Bergkamp, to matches in Europe. 'I was his accomplice,' Akers laughs. Scott proved to be a slightly less sociable companion. 'I had my headphones on in the back of the car pretending I was asleep,' she laughs. The R'n'B fanatic had planned to hobble to the changing rooms to congratulate the girls on their 1-0 win that night, but Akers and Donnelly were ready for the off from Zwolle the moment the whistle had blown. 'I was gutted, I drove all that way and didn't even see the girls,' she shrugs.

It took Scott until February 2006 to see off the first major injury of her career and she returned for Arsenal in an FA Cup quarter-final victory over London rivals Chelsea. Scott came off the bench for England against Iceland in March and was still among the substitutes come the visit from Hungary two months later. Not surprisingly then, both Scott and Exley are eager to impress as 8,817 fans and a BBC3 audience take in the game at St Mary's. Exley's determination to make an impact on her forty-seventh cap shows itself within ten minutes of the kick-off. Melinda Szvorda does well to tip over the Donny midfielder's swerving free-kick from thirty yards. Her long-time England colleague Sue Smith is just as keen to justify her place in the starting XI and she controls a bad clearance on the edge of the box seven minutes later and skips past three defenders but her enthusiasm gets the better of her and she shoots wide and high. Undeterred, Smith keeps plugging away and whips in a fantastic cross from the right to find Anita Asante unmarked in front of goal but her clever side-foot shot is tipped onto the post by Szvorda. It is not all one-way traffic, though, and Szvorda's opposite number Rachel Brown is called into action just before the break, diving to catch a shot by Anett Nagy from the edge of the area after a Hungary free-kick ricochets off the wall. England respond as Rachel Unitt feeds Karen Carney on the edge of the area only to see the teenager bundled over by Éva Sümegi before she can get a shot away. Up steps Exley to take command of the ball and the Donny captain proves her worth as her neatly struck free-kick swings around the wall from twenty yards and into the bottom corner. It is a classy goal. 'My first home goal out of the six I've scored,' Exley declares. A furious end to the half sees Carney narrowly miss out on one herself, her cross-cum-shot rebounding off the post. But when England troop into the changing rooms at half-time, Powell is far from happy and asks the team to tell her what the problem is. Substitute Scott has run the rule on the game and answers the question, announcing, 'It doesn't look like anyone wants to perform, everyone's waiting for someone else to do something.'

It is an insight that galvanises the team and defender Faye White, recording her half-century of caps, leads by example at the restart when she launches herself into the attack and heads just over from Sue Smith's dangerous cross. The woodwork starts to take a battering as England raise their game, knowing full well how much is at stake. Scott has been itching to get on and does so when she replaces her room-mate Carney in midfield in the fifty-seventh minute. Powell has a word in Scott's ear as she prepares to enter the field, but all eyes are on Brown who has to dive to keep out Ágnes Czuder's first-time shot. Teenage substitute and senior-side debutante Lianne Sanderson of Arsenal is soon making a nuisance of herself up at the other end, heading Scott's cross straight at the goalkeeper before magnificently controlling a Unitt throw-in on her chest and hitting the bar from twenty-two yards. Her old Arsenal teammate Jo Potter gets the crowd going with a bristling shot that skims the side netting and Scott floats the ball goalward but only manages to add to England's woodwork-bashing tally. The substitute makes no mistake in stoppage time. A clever back-heel from Sanderson sees Sue Smith power down the left wing before crossing for Scott to head coolly home at the far post. It is a far cry from 13-0 but another clean sheet and three more points are enough to keep Powell happy.

Come full-time, Scott's colleagues find out what Powell had whispered in the ear of her player. 'She said, "You're going to go on and you're going to score for me",' laughs Scott, who had left her goal late, but had done enough to regain her starting berth for England's next date – a much more daunting visit from a Holland side that will need finishing off long before the final whistle.

Staying Power

The pressure is well and truly on England going into the penultimate match of their campaign. Facing Holland at The Valley in a game that is to go out on live television may have prompted a ripple of nervousness to pass through the camp. But the main preoccupation of the England squad ahead of the match is not how they will look on the telly; they are more concerned with seeing off the only side to have put a spanner in the works of group favourites France's qualification bid. Holland had beaten France and only just succumbed to England in their previous meeting nine months ago, a 1-0 loss at home. A mere handful of places separated the two teams in the world rankings by August 2006, with England rated twelfth and Holland seventeenth. England midfielder Fara Williams, who scored the only goal in the away match back in November 2005, admitted the squad recognised Holland were no pushovers. 'Knowing they had beaten France we knew it was going to be a test,' she says. What is more, it would be one England would have to face without their captain.

Arsenal and England skipper Faye White had endured a patchy campaign thus far. Having played just two full games, the England no.5 had missed the winter friendlies against Sweden with an ankle injury. Suspension for the grudge home match with France saw Hope Powell leave the defender on the bench for the warm-up game against Iceland. Regardless of those enforced no-shows, she returned to lead the side twice more and still had the final two games well within her sights as the tail end of the qualifiers approached. Indeed,

White was so set on playing her part in those crunch ties, she had turned down the chance of a stint with Hammarby and the elite of the Swedish league. 'That summer I nearly went to play in Sweden,' she recalls. 'But I thought no, I won't take it because I've got two big games, England could qualify for the World Cup and I want to be part of that.' So 'Debs', as White is known at Arsenal, stayed at home in Hertfordshire and threw herself into pre-season training with her club. Their first friendly on 16 July 2006 saw the league champions take on Bristol City. It also saw White's season finish before it had even begun. A thump on the knee left the defender sick to her stomach and barely able to stand, let alone run. The then twenty-eight-year-old would play no further part in England's World Cup qualification adventure; she had suffered the injury every player dreads, a ruptured cruciate ligament.

It was not a new experience for White. In mid-November 2002, England were due to face France away in their bid to make it to the World Cup 2003. White had been elevated to the Arsenal captaincy three weeks previously and was in Premier League action against London rivals Fulham. Throwing her weight into a clearance in the penalty area while defending a corner, White collided with her goalkeeper Emma Byrne and a couple of Fulham forwards. Cautiously dragging herself to her feet after tumbling awkwardly on the turf, White attempted to carry on. It was impossible. 'I got up and tried to run after Rachel Yankey, couldn't and thought, oh I'm going to be sick,' she recalls. Scans later revealed that White had come out of the challenge with a ruptured left anterior cruciate ligament. It was a week before the make-or-break return leg against World Cup play-off favourites France in St Etienne.

So when an ashen faced White felt the same kind of 'moving' sensation while attacking a corner in the pre-season friendly against Bristol four years later, she dreaded to think that the same career-threatening injury had struck again, this time to her right knee. 'On the pitch I had a gut feeling,' she recalls. 'That night when I got home, I got out of the car and put my weight on it and was nearly sick.' It was scarcely seven weeks before England were due to take on Holland and though White tried to stay upbeat, the scan results confirmed her worst suspicions. She says:

> I was saying it won't be, it will be... I was trying to be positive about the injury. But Vic came in and I said, 'Hi are you all right?' And he said, 'Yes, but you're not going to be,' then he was straight on the phone saying we'll see the surgeon.

The 'Vic' in question is Vic Akers, manager and founder of Arsenal Ladies back in 1987. The Gunners boss, who doubles as kit manager for the men's team, signed White from Southern Division side Three Bridges in 1996. 'She was a big figure in their team and the potential that she had was apparent,' he recalls. In the intervening years, the Arsenal manager has seen the player develop from dependable central defender to Arsenal and England captain and role model to aspiring girls at grassroots level. 'I remember meeting her at a McDonalds at Gatwick Airport,' says Akers, recalling his initial discussions with the player as she sought to move into the Premier League elite. Like many of her peers, the England hopeful had been encouraged to step up to the Premier League's National Division for the good of her international career. As England entered the final stages of their World Cup 2007 qualification campaign, White was entering her eleventh season at the north London club. 'Not many players leave this club and that's a good sign of what's going on within it,' says Akers. 'A lot may moan and have the hump with me at times but you rarely see many want to leave because they know it's the best.' By that season, however, Akers wanted to prove FA Cup and League champions Arsenal were the best in Europe as well as at home and he had come into pre-season in optimistic mood. The former Cambridge United and Watford defender had just landed three key signings on and off the field. Former reservist Emma Hayes had returned to the club as his second in command after an award-winning spell coaching in America's college and

W-League set-ups. On the pitch, England's midfield enforcer Katie Chapman had switched from London rivals Charlton and teenage winger Karen Carney had signed from Birmingham City. Their arrival meant the Gunners' team sheet now read like the who's who of top-flight women's football. Arsenal boasted seven of England's Euro 2005 starting XI on their roster along with Wales captain Jayne Ludlow and Scotland skipper Julie Fleeting plus at least two of the most promising youngsters then on the fringes of the England senior team, livewire striker Lianne Sanderson and versatile midfielder cum defender Anita Asante.

It was a set-up that would not only benefit Arsenal, but the England team as well according to Gunner Mary Phillip. 'Having so many international players in your club is obviously great for the national team because you get to know each other that bit more in the team,' she said. The season was hardly two weeks old when Arsenal played Fulham, the side Phillip used to captain as a professional. Recently set adrift by their men's side, the weakened club were battered 14-0. It was a result that elicited little joy within the league given that Fulham had been treble winners just a few years previously. But scoring so confidently a mere four days before England were due to face Holland, goal-getter Kelly Smith reckoned it would at least benefit Powell's side going into the match. 'It breeds confidence coming into camp when you get so many goals in a game,' she said.

Few disagreed, but a return to double-figure victories in the league hardly inspired confidence of a closely-fought season in the newly expanded twelve-club National Division. Arsenal's international monopoly sparked lively debate from that match forward. 'So many Arsenal players – is that a good thing or a bad thing for the league?' mused Hope Powell in one England press conference. 'Is the league conducive to international football? Those are certain questions that we have to look at.' While the powers that be at the FA continue to mull over the issue, those involved in the women's game can only second guess possible solutions, including summer or mid-week leagues that could allow clubs to generate their own income,

Despite the loss of captain Faye White to injury, Arsenal still provide seven players for the home qualifier against Holland. From left to right: Karen Carney, Anita Asante, Rachel Yankey, Mary Phillip, Alex Scott, Katie Chapman and Kelly Smith.

attract new players and garner greater attention from broadcasters and journalists. Get one too many walkovers in a season and you could have fans and the media reaching for the off button. 'It would be nice if there was an evenly based amount of players at each club so the league becomes stronger,' says former England striker and occasional BBC commentator Marieanne Spacey. 'Television doesn't want to go to a game where it's 10-0. If there was an even spread of the internationals, it makes the league stronger and makes it a better product to sell to television.'

Yet imposing an equal share of the best players could be impossible given the mostly amateur status of the game. Clubs such as Charlton and Arsenal enjoy backing from the men's side that allows them to attract players with semi-professional terms. But at the opposite end of the spectrum, there are teams such as Manchester United, Leeds, Fulham, Southampton and Cardiff City whose ties with their parent clubs have been severed. It is a situation that has not escaped the notice of the England skipper and in giving evidence to the House of Commons Select Committee into women's football she said:

> ...although it is slowly closing, there is a big gulf between the top teams that get everything and are well supported and the ones that are struggling. We are fortunate to have over six people employed to run the ladies' team, but many of the lower clubs do not have that luxury as well and that affects everything from how you market a game to the training facilities and the running of the club.

Indeed, Arsenal FC have offered their star female attractions jobs at the club since the turn of this century. The current crop are no exception, with Kelly Smith employed as assistant director of the Arsenal Ladies academy and qualified sports massage therapist Faye White working alongside Irish international Ciara Grant in the women's football development office. But the club's longest-serving player also insists Arsenal's support is hard won:

> It's up to other clubs and players to work just as hard as people who work here to make that happen. Because until you see what people do, you just think, 'Oh they're lucky, they get everything' and it's like no, it's not the case, it's someone driving it who has the passion and tenacity to keep doing it no matter how many things they win, they still want to get better, they still want to drive it forwards.

By 2006, Akers was keen to propel Arsenal to the one title he had yet to deliver since forming the Ladies in 1987 – the UEFA Cup. Before his summer holiday suntan had even begun to fade, Akers declared, 'We are in four major tournaments, our aims are to win all four and that doesn't change from year to year, but we know Europe is the biggest headache.' As it turned out, Arsenal did overcome that particular challenge in April 2007, making it all the way to the UEFA Cup final where they beat Swedish champions Umeå. Losing White for almost the entire season was, however, a pain the manager could have done without, even if he did have the woman he dubs as his future captain, Anita Asante, to fill the void. England would look to the up-and-coming Asante to shore up the heart of their defence too. And as the university graduate did so, White could only look on.

It was not a task that sat particularly easily with the Sussex-born player. Since taking up the game as an eight-year-old with her older brother Steven, White has not been one for sitting and watching. Getting stuck in on the pitch with the boys and coming home with her regulation school skirt in tatters was more the gawky schoolgirl's style as White recalls:

> I used to run out at school every break time to go and play football with the boys... I had a really tight skirt and used to yank it right up and hold it and every night I'd go home with it ripped or dirty and my mum used to be sewing it all the time.

The towering tomboy swapped her skirt for shorts a couple of years later when she talked her way into training sessions at Steven's club Horley Town Minors, in a team run by her dad Trevor. Those kick-abouts with the lads gave her a first taste of competitive football, even though the only girl in the team never actually ran out for the club. 'I'd be one of the boys pretty much, apart from playing on the Sunday,' she says. 'I just used to run on with the oranges at half-time. That was my job, I was so lucky!' White thought her good fortune really had run out by the time she hit thirteen, though. Fearing for her safety as his daughter punched above her weight on the pitch against fifteen- and sixteen-year-old lads, Trevor told her it was time to stop playing with the team. His daughter disagreed. 'Some of the challenges I used to go in for, the boys would come off hurting more than I would,' she says. Trevor White eventually brought his daughter around to his way of thinking, though, and just a few weeks later, White was glad her dad had.

News of a soccer camp in Crawley Leisure Centre filtered through to White and the teenager donned her football kit and rolled up to the venue with her mum Christine at her side. Standing there in shorts and shirt, White was the only girl in the entire sports hall.

As luck would have it, the female coach running the course was the reserve-team manager for local women's side Horsham. Within a year, White had finally tasted competitive action and was soon lapping it up with the first team amid the rough and tumble of the Premier League's Southern Division. White's football education continued apace off the pitch during this time too. Unlike many of her current international teammates who confess to not even knowing an England women's team existed, White knew all about the national team and wanted a piece of that action too. The seventeen-year-old had stayed awake until the early hours of the morning in the summer of 1995 just to catch a brief ten-minute slot on the television detailing the progress of England in the World Cup in Sweden. It may have only been a fleeting glimpse of Ted Copeland's squad but it was enough to set White on the road to the World Cup herself. 'When I saw them on the telly, I was right that's what I want to do,' she says. She was about to do it sooner than she had imagined.

White was still a relative fledgling when Copeland decided to take a closer look at the player. The England team's agonising World Cup quarter-final defeat to Germany was just three months old when White was invited along to a Bisham Abbey training camp. She was more than a little excited at the prospect:

> I got a letter through the door saying you've been selected for England and I was just like, oh my godMy heart was bumping, I remember it, it was beating out of my chest and I was just like, I don't want to open it and then I did and saw the names that would be going, you know, Marieanne [Spacey], Gill [Coultard], Hope [Powell], Debbie Bampton – all the players that were in the top league that I wasn't even playing in.

Getting to grips with the first meal of the day was tricky enough during that initial try-out. 'I was so nervous going into breakfast,' she laughs, recalling how she was the only player from outside the National Division to be called up. But that status only lasted one more season. Realising she needed to move up a league, the ambitious player organised a switch. As Debbie Bampton's Croydon were south of the river, the club managed by the then England captain was the obvious choice for the Sussex-based player. But Bampton was away on holiday while White was working on her move, and in the interim she met up with Akers. Then on the brink of his tenth season as Arsenal boss, the ex-professional footballer knew how to push all the right buttons to land the player for his squad. He duly drove down to meet White over a cup of tea at Gatwick Airport before paying a visit to her (Tottenham supporting) parents. Then came the masterstroke – Akers ushered the player to Highbury to watch a training session from a comfy executive box in the stands of the hallowed north London ground. 'The door opened and it was just like oh, okay then, yeah right, I might play for you,' she recalls. 'He just made you feel like he wanted you.'

White swapped her rusty orange kit of Three Bridges for the red and white of Arsenal that season of 1996/97 and had won the league by the end of it. But a first title was not the only thing she collected that term. She also picked up a reputation as the leggy new kid on the block that few players wanted to come up against. 'I remember thinking this girl is difficult to get around if you don't get away from her,' says Hope Powell, recalling her battles with White when Arsenal faced off against Croydon that season. 'She used to get on my nerves.' White did not quite manage to put her long limbs in the way of Wembley's progress to the FA Cup final that year, though. A slip-up against Tracy Koch in the semi-final at Boreham Wood FC saw the north-west London side crush Arsenal's double dreams. 'Their striker and me clashed and I fell over and she carried on running and scored a goal and we lost 1-0,' White grimaces. 'It was my first FA Cup experience. I was distraught.' White did not feel much happier about her first England appearance, at Sheffield United, that year either. The teenager came on as Ted Copeland threw all five of his substitutes on against Scotland in a 6-0 victory. 'I had a stinker, was awful,' she says. White had not completely messed up, though, and was understandably eager to make a better impression when her first full cap arrived in February 1998, less than two weeks after her twentieth birthday. France won that friendly in Alençon 3-2 but White put in a solid enough display at the centre of England's defence to win Player of the Match plaudits. 'I'd been around the squad without going straight into it so I was like, am I good enough? I don't know,' she admits. 'Then I got Player of the Match and I was like, yes! I was so determined to do well and to prove to everyone and myself that I was good enough to play.'

In the years that followed, White could do no wrong domestically. Voted the Express Sport and Nike Premier League Player of the Year during the 1997/98 season of FA and League cup triumphs for Arsenal, within three more years she had tucked two more FA Cups, three League Cups and a League title under her belt. But while White was one of the first names on Akers' team sheet, she had not yet become new England manager Hope Powell's first choice. Around this time, Powell had Mo Marley at the heart of her defensive set-up alongside a teenage Katie Chapman. So unlike contemporaries Sue Smith and Chapman, White spent most of this period, including all but one game of Euro 2001 in Germany, warming the England bench. 'She was upset that she was not playing,' recalls Powell of the Euros. 'I joke with her about it now but she just says, "I was young".' Humour was mum and dad's way of lifting the defender out of the doldrums too. 'My family always used to joke, "You did the best warm-up tonight" and we used to have a laugh about it in the end,' she says. It was hard to always maintain a sense of humour, though. She says:

> At Arsenal, I started every game, I've never been a sub, whereas with England I would go and I would sit there… I remember sometimes I'd be in the stand, wouldn't even be on the bench and you'd be like, I still want to play and I feel part of it so that's good but maybe I'm not good enough or what else do I have to do?

The answer to that question was to bide her time. The England no.12 did get on the pitch in the final Euro match, against Germany, and Powell recalls reassuring the defender. 'I remember saying your time will come, you're just not ready,' she says. Powell told White to go

Euro 2001 provides Faye White (12) with a starting block for her England career just as Arsenal teammate Marieanne Spacey (16) calls time on hers.

away and work on her game, particularly her heading. It paid off. When thirty-something Mo Marley retired from the international scene after Euro 2001 along with striker Marieanne Spacey, Powell looked to White to fill the void. The Arsenal defender knew she had to seize the opportunity to finally make an impression with England. 'I was just like, right this is my chance, I've got to prove it,' she says.

A couple of months later, White landed the chance to do just that. It was a baptism of fire, though. Facing Denmark in the first match since a disappointing Euro display, White and her England colleagues were on the receiving end of a 3-0 reverse. It did not get much easier as they went into qualification matches for the upcoming World Cup 2003. But White cemented her place in the starting XI as England recorded a loss to Euro champions Germany, and a draw and victory over both Portugal and Holland. By spring 2002, Powell had not just offered White the chance to wear an England shirt; she had offered her the carrot of the captaincy too. White recalls:

> We played Germany at Crystal Palace… Just before I walked out she stopped me in the corridor and just said, 'You could be the next England captain, I need you to show me over the next few months, that's what I have in mind for you.' And I was like, oh my god.

White still has not figured out what Powell saw in her at this time. 'I was never really the loudest player in the squad or the one that was always certain to start so for me it was quite hard to think why are you picking me?' she says. 'But I'm quite focused and driven and will say things if I need to.' Powell knows exactly what she saw in the central defender. 'The way that she prepares for matches, I thought this girl is a natural leader, she doesn't care whether she is popular or not, she has a real future in the game,' the manager says. It was only a matter of months before Powell put her instinct to the test. In July 2002, White was given the armband by England captain and veteran striker Karen Walker at half-time and walked out for the second half against Nigeria at Norwich City FC to the applause of 8,034 fans, including her parents and grandad Arthur. 'I was in the boardroom having a sandwich, someone said Kaz Walker was not coming out the second half and I said to my dad, I bet Faye comes out as captain and there she was, with the armband sort of hidden under her shirt,' recalls Trevor White. His daughter wore the elasticated band more prominently two months later when Walker's suspension for a crucial World Cup play-off semi-final against Iceland saw the defender lead her country from first whistle. Striding out of the tunnel as 7,019 fans enthusiastically welcomed the women's side to Birmingham City's St Andrew's stadium almost took White's breath away. 'It was brilliant,' she says. 'Suddenly you get another 125 per cent energy. I was running around like I could have run around for the next twenty years.' Powell's team went on to win that match against Iceland 1-0, with a late, late goal from Amanda Barr. The result set up the World Cup 2003 play-off final encounters with France, which saw Walker resume the captaincy. Come the crucial second leg, the Doncaster Belle would lead the team without her understudy. White was back on the sidelines having just suffered her first knee ligament injury.

Arsenal defender Sol Campbell was among those who descended on the player's hospital room in an effort to chivvy her along following keyhole surgery to repair the rupture on Christmas Eve 2002. Campbell told his Arsenal counterpart to keep her chin up, but he had no doubts about the then fitness instructor's determination to make it back on to the pitch. Neither did her family. 'I remember picking her up from the hospital on Christmas Eve,' says her dad. 'We had fun and games getting her up and down the stairs because she couldn't put too much weight on the leg but she didn't need much pushing because she was focused on getting back.' That feat was achieved in the early weeks of the 2003/04 season, but only after six months of gruelling strengthening exercises at home and later in the gym and in the local park with boyfriend Keith. Breaking her nose in her first game back, a friendly against Athletic Bilbao, was not the best of starts. Bilbao's physiotherapist deftly cracked White's nose back into place on the pitch and the player was soon back to her combative self. But it was not just the Arsenal captaincy that White had reclaimed. Following the international retirement of the popular and well-grounded Yorkshire striker Karen Walker, White was confirmed as England skipper by October as well. In her first game back she led the side to a 2-2 draw with Russia in Moscow. A revitalised White then capped an impressive return to home soil by bagging two goals and the Player of the Match champagne in a 5-0 win over Scotland at Preston North End's ground three weeks later. It was a stirring comeback that was mirrored domestically too.

Come May 2004, White held the FA Cup aloft in front of 12,244 fans and a BBC1 audience of 2.2 million following Arsenal and Scotland striker Julie Fleeting's hat-trick in a demolition of Charlton at a rainy Loftus Road. Less than a fortnight later, White paraded the League championship trophy to 5,000 cheering Gooners and her Arsenal mentor Sol Campbell at Highbury. Vic Akers' side had clinched the title in a tense final-day decider at the men's ground that was later rewarded with an open-topped bus tour around Islington alongside Arsenal's Premiership-winning men.

Arsenal manager Vic Akers congratulates captain Faye White after a victorious display in the FA Cup final 2004.

Faye White looks at home chatting to presenter Manish Bhasin (left) and Manchester United legend Gary Pallister (right) on the BBC's *Football Focus.*

By the time Euro 2005 came around in Manchester and Blackburn, just a few miles down the road from the scene of that Deepdale triumph over Scotland, the then twenty-seven-year-old White had led Arsenal to yet another League title and sealed a League Cup final victory over rivals Charlton with a long-range thunderbolt of a goal at Brentford FC's Griffin Park. Ahead of the Euros, White starred on *Football Focus* and received words of encouragement from David Beckham, her counterpart in the national men's side. In the aftermath, she appeared on *A Question of Sport* and would go on to be awarded an MBE for her promotion of the game. The England centre-back had little trouble adjusting to the limelight. 'Sometimes you feel like you're putting yourself on the stage all the time but then if you don't do it, how is the sport going to grow?' she asks. 'When I was younger, looking up to players and having them to draw on was great.' But even if White was eager to talk up the game to the public, commentating to a live television audience was not what the skipper had in mind when she had envisaged England playing their penultimate World Cup qualifier. Unfortunately, it was the best she was going to get, having been forced back onto crutches just months after collecting the FA Cup for League champions Arsenal at the New Den following an unforgiving 5-0 victory over a Leeds side that featured former England captain Karen Walker.

White was not the only one battling disappointment as a determined England stomped their way on to Charlton Athletic's pitch at The Valley in front of 7,931 fans that August evening. Despite an excellent showing in the previous match against Hungary, Leeds midfielder Sue Smith was back picking the mud from her studs on the bench. 'I just kept quiet and played as well as I could in training,' Smith shrugs. 'Mentally I was so much stronger after the Euros and just put it behind me.' The team were tougher too by all accounts. In the aftermath of the France home game in March, the group felt their approach to the tie had been off beam. 'We thought we were quite defensive and instead of playing a 4-3-3 and pushing on, we thought we sat back in 4-5-1,' recalls midfielder Fara Williams. 'We concentrated on their strengths rather than ours.' White says that before

Former England captain Karen Walker (centre, white shirt) greets her successor Faye White before the Arsenal *v.* Leeds FA Cup final in 2006.

Holland came calling, therefore, the squad had told their coaches they wanted to try a change of tack. 'Before that game they had had meetings and said to the coaches, "We need to look at attacking",' she says. 'They had an input and Hope took it on board.' Powell responded to their concerns with a call for her team to go out at The Valley and express themselves. They took her on her word.

Facing England on the final day of August 2006, the Dutch attempt to prove they are not just here to make up numbers. They enjoy an early chance but skipper Mary Phillip manages to halt the run of birthday girl Manon Melis, who was twenty that day. The stand-in captain makes a telling contribution again eight minutes later, lofting a cross towards Kelly Smith who brings the ball down on her chest, bypasses two defenders and smashes the ball in the bottom corner to open the scoring. The omnipresent Kelly Smith has the bit between her teeth and wins a penalty just before the twenty-five-minute mark, coolly sending the goalie the wrong way as she dispatches the spot kick before pounding the turf with her fist in celebration. There is no respite for keeper Marleen Wissink who has to remain on her toes to deny Smith a hat-trick, beating away her stinging shot just before half-time. England go into the break knowing their performance is a far cry from the last time they met Holland even if there is still work to do.

Kelly Smith cannot wait to get down to it, though, and five minutes into the restart the former USA women's league professional wraps up her hat-trick with a left-foot volley that is deflected off Karen Carney's back and loops into the net. Smith races to the England dug-out to hug her manager but it is her absent colleague and house-mate who will be acknowledged by the player afterwards – the hat-trick heroine dedicating her goals to the injured Faye White. 'I live with her so see the struggles that she goes through day in and day out and her training habits and routine,' Smith says. 'I thought it might give her a bit of a boost.' But Smith's influence on the game is not over and on sixty-seven minutes, she wins a free-kick that Rachel Yankey runs over to take. Smith trots away to find herself completely unmarked in the box and screams at her Arsenal teammate for the ball. The moment is lost and Smith wheels away in frustration but turns back in a dance of delight seconds later. Yankey has whipped the ball over Wissink's head and into the top far corner. The winger puts her hand over her mouth to stifle a giggle before rubbing her hands as her teammates, including Smith, rush towards her with their congratulations. Jigging merrily in England's goalmouth, Rachel Brown is a long way off the celebrations, but understands all too well the significance of the victory. 'Scoring four goals past a team that was causing problems when we played them away was a great confidence boost for us,' she says afterwards. Over in the studio where she is analysing the game with Sky's Clare Tomlinson, White can hardly contain her delight. 'I would have loved to have played in that game,' she says. 'Everything clicked. It's as if the girls thought, "We stood up and said something we believe in and now we have to make sure we deliver".' In a month's time, they would get one last chance to deliver the one thing they were all striving for – a World Cup berth. All eyes now were on France.

All or Nothing

As the last day of September 2006 dawned, Hope Powell's England awoke in Brittany knowing they were ninety minutes of football away from qualification for the biggest tournament of their lives – the World Cup. England had always feared that the battle for that one desperately-sought qualification spot would be settled in the final game against favourites France on foreign soil. They also believed that the goals they had been pumping into their opponents' nets during the campaign could play a part should things not go to plan. How wrong they were. UEFA rules meant head-to-head results between France and England during the campaign and not goal difference would come into play first should they finish neck and neck on points. So, after the draw at Blackburn and with France three points behind England, the home side just needed a win against their rivals in this final match to take the World Cup spot the two sides were vying for. That was despite the visitors' supremely better goal difference of 27 to France's 11.

The news hit the England players like a bolt from the blue. 'Head-to-head was like a wicked rumour,' says keeper Rachel Brown. Her manager acknowledged the rule was set in stone but was still baffled by it. 'It's absolutely ridiculous,' Powell told the press at Soho Square beforehand. 'We've won this group, right? We've won it. If you look at it, we've won the group. We could lose to France – we've won the group but we won't qualify. It's ridiculous. I can't even go there. It's absolutely ridiculous. But who am I to say it's ridiculous?' It was not just the thought of a quirky rule that fired England up for this final match, however, those old memories of St Etienne came flooding back too. Midfielder Fara Williams was adamant there would be no repeat of that defeat. 'The French were so arrogant,' she recalls. 'I was not going out on that pitch and losing that game and letting them laugh.' But there were some who battled to stay positive as nerves took hold. Sue Smith recalls:

> Not qualifying last time was awful. We were talking about it before the France game, I said to Mary Phillip, I can't see us getting beaten but I can't see us qualifying and she said she felt the same because all we remembered was getting knocked out. It was difficult for a few of us to stay positive and focused.

Of any player, though, Phillip was best equipped to gee up her team. Having worn the captain's armband in the absence of injured skipper Faye White, Phillip offered not only leadership but an insight into what England would be missing out on if they failed to return home with the correct result.

Back in 1995, the last time England played in the World Cup, the defender had tasted a 'Theo Walcott' moment. Like her Arsenal club counterpart Walcott in the men's World Cup 2006, a teenage Phillip was a surprise addition to her country's roster. The then Millwall player had only ever pulled on an England training jersey before international manager Ted Copeland decided to add her to his World Cup squad list for Sweden. 'It was an opportunity to take younger players to a major tournament which could provide them with valuable experience both in the short and long term,' says Copeland, looking back. But with just that solo appearance at a weekend England camp in Maidenhead under her belt, Phillip was as surprised as the rest of the women's game at her inclusion. Like Walcott, however, the eighteen-year-old was not about to set the world alight that summer. She had to make do with a view from the sidelines as England, featuring future manager Powell, made it as far as the quarter-finals where they went out to Germany. It did not stop her from drinking in the atmosphere in Sweden as she mingled with the best players from across the world. 'I was called in at the last minute at eighteen and I was only part of the squad,' she recalls. 'I saw how the set-up was and how things worked but I wasn't actually part of that team and probably never had a chance to get on the field.' The pragmatic mother of two insists, however, that simply attending the biggest tournament in the women's game set her in good stead for a career that had netted her 49 caps on the eve of the final World Cup 2007 qualifying match against France. 'I didn't feel I was actually going to go out and play,' she admits. 'But it was great to be in that squad and be involved in the England set-up at such a young age.'

It is a view that Phillip's Arsenal colleague Anita 'Neets' Asante can fully appreciate. Asante was just twenty when she was called up to fulfil England's midfield quota for Euro 2005. Manager Hope Powell had left out established names like Sue Smith, Rachel McArthur and Kristy Moore to make room for a new breed of younger players that she felt had outperformed their older rivals when a squad of thirty battled to be part of the final Euro band of twenty. Asante's England Under-19 colleagues Eni Aluko and Karen Carney seized the chance to reveal their youthful capabilities on the European stage during the competition. But degree student Asante, who was returning from a knee injury and sitting exams, had to be content with watching from the dugouts amid thousands of yelling fans at the City of Manchester Stadium and Ewood Park. 'Not really playing saddened her,' says her mum Tina. Like Phillip in the World Cup 1995, however, the England no.17 took only positives. 'I just kept working, didn't dwell on it, thought, I'm just going to keep pushing on from here,' she says. Despite her tender years, it was not Asante's only England knock-back. The versatile player – Asante has covered every position bar goalkeeper in her time – was overlooked the first time she tried out for her national side. Once she was finally involved, Asante had to be content with a substitute's bib for all but one match of the Under-19 World Cup in Canada in 2002. But that never-say-die attitude would serve her well right up to the last-gasp World Cup 2007 qualifying tie in France. Filling in for Faye White at central defence alongside Mary Phillip in that tense final game, the twenty-one-year-old would go on to win rave Player of the Match reviews. It was the kind of achievement Asante could only have dreamt of a few years earlier when she was kicking around a metal-encased football pitch with boys in north-west London.

Being snapped up by Arsenal defender Clare Wheatley and striker Rachel Yankey at a football development session at the age of thirteen was the start of Asante's rise up the women's ranks. But the player Arsene Wenger compares to defender Kolo Touré had already learnt the basics in a much less structured fashion – playing with lads on a pitch she dubs 'the cage' near her home in Edgware. Dashing to the cage after school each night, the Liverpool FC-supporting youngster learned how to win a tackle, see a pass and score a goal with as much aplomb as the male Premiership players she and her friends admired. 'For me, it was about showing your skills,' she says. 'It was, can you beat that player with a skill that no one has seen or as a team, can you look like Arsenal men with the flair? I used to love it.'

Tennis became another big love once Asante arrived at Mill Hill County High School. From chess to football, sport was high on the agenda at the north London school whose alumni include former Arsenal men's vice-chairman and women's chairman David Dein. There, Asante threw herself into those sporting traditions, fitting lawn tennis training around her habitual evening matches in the cage. But with the encouragement of physical education head Jan Harding, Asante fitted school football into her busy sporting calendar too. Running out for Mill Hill's girls' team gave Asante the chance to compete in a more organised fashion than street football offered; it also allowed her to discover a side to the game she never knew existed – that girls can play too. 'Every girl out there thinks they are the only girl playing,' she says. 'You have no idea about the women's football movement.' Asante caught a glimpse of it when she came up against Queens Park School from Brent and their star player Eartha

Anita Asante shines in defence or midfield for the Gunners.

Pond. She recalls, 'I thought, oh this is cool, there's another player with talent.' Charlton defender Pond recognised Asante's potential from the off as well. 'Anita has always been strong and confident on the ball so I'm not surprised she is where she is today,' Pond says.

Urged on by Jan Harding, the teenage Asante came across even more female players with skills to match her own in the form of the Arsenal Ladies. The names of Gunners Rachel Yankey and Clare Wheatley meant nothing when, in 1998, Asante gingerly stepped into one of their football development sessions in the London suburb of Burnt Oak. She would go on to play alongside them after her tough tackling and clean passing gave her the first foothold on the Arsenal ladder: an invite to their centre of excellence. 'I remember looking at her at this little development session thinking, that player has got to be with a club so I've got to speak with the manager,' recalls former

England defender Wheatley. 'When I spoke to her and she said she wasn't with anybody and just played in a back yard or at school I was gobsmacked. She was completely raw in terms of coaching but technically better than any other raw talent I've ever seen.'

Evenings spent performing drills and playing practice games with the Arsenal elite in the north-east London borough of Hackney meant it was game, set and match for tennis. But abandoning games in the cage and challenges to impromptu matches with men and boys in the local park took slightly longer. 'It came to a point when I realised I can't do this every week,' she says. 'But I think it helps girls when you are young because it's that concept of street football that you can't always find at centres of excellence. It toughens you up as well, you want to show them that you're good enough.'

Before long, Asante was looking to impress in a different kind of football environment entirely. An invitation to the stately surroundings of Bisham Abbey arrived at the Mill Hill schoolgirl's home not long after she had been elevated to Arsenal's Under-16 squad. It was a thrilling call-up. The only problem was plenty of other girls had danced around their front rooms in delight at having received an invite too. 'There were a couple of hundred kids and I was nervous,' she recalls. 'That was my first time of knowing anything about England.' Asante's jitters told as she attempted to show some of the skills she had learnt on the streets to the keen-eyed England coaches. The next letter to arrive on the family doormat was one informing the Asantes' eldest of three children that she had not made the grade. Tina Asante remembers telling her daughter not to give up. 'We kept reassuring her that her time would come,' recalls Tina, a nurse who never wearies of telling the doctors she works with about her football-playing daughter.

Mum was right and there were no disappointed faces in the Asante household after a second trial invite yielded the GCSE student the chance to travel north for an Under-17 tournament in Scotland. That trip saw the budding England players face teams from the home nation, plus Northern Ireland and the US. It was a toe in the water that has become the stuff of folklore among the England hopefuls who attended. 'We still talk about it now,' says Asante. The 'we' in question includes Eni Aluko, her room-mate in the senior England team and, until 2006 when Asante graduated, a fellow Brunel University student. Get the two together and there is rarely a dull moment. 'She's a very intelligent girl so we have very good conversations about things that interest us and at the same time we appreciate our differing opinions,' says Aluko. But teammates who walk in on the pair during their down time on international duty are just as likely to find the two stumbling around the room in search of Aluko's missing sock as hotly debating current affairs. 'I always tell her, Eni, I feel like I'm babysitting you,' Asante laughs. 'She's the worst person for remembering her kit, her boots, shin pads, one sock, but we have a laugh and get on really well.'

Like her room-mate, Asante went on to serve her apprenticeship in England's Under-19s and newly formed Under-21s. A substitute appearance in the Under-19 World Cup 2002 was only marginal headway. Asante came on for eight minutes against Chinese Taipei, as England advanced to the quarter-finals where the young Lionesses faced a partisan crowd of 23,595 who roared hosts Canada to victory at the Edmonton Commonwealth Stadium. The chance to finally prove herself in tournament play came with starting berths in four Under-19 European Championship 2003 matches in Germany alongside Aluko, Alex Scott, Fara Williams and Jo Potter. Again the young England players were edged out – falling in the semi-finals to France. Missing out on the finals of that annual competition the following April brought disappointment to the camp and their first-choice midfielder. But it was all forgotten in the hectic month of May. After coming up through the ranks, degree student Asante played her part as Arsenal lifted the FA Cup with victory over Charlton at Loftus Road and snatched the League title at Highbury from their other London rivals, Fulham. Just a day before that nail-biting season finale, Asante had gained her first call-up for Hope Powell's seniors. Exams had forced Everton's Kelly McDougall to

Anita Asante has starred for England at youth and senior levels.

pull out of the England squad ahead of their friendly against Iceland at Peterborough FC and the Arsenal midfielder was drafted into the squad in her place. But Asante did not just sit on the bench, she got the chance to run out in a senior shirt at London Road in a 1-0 victory over the visitors. It was not just an important day for Anita Asante, though. Tina Asante was not used to driving long distances back then but made an exception when it came to collecting her daughter the night she won her first senior cap. Like Anita, Tina has never looked back. 'I didn't drive anywhere other than Edgware,' laughs Tina. 'My first long journey was driving to Peterborough to pick her up, I was quite pleased with myself. It helped me drive far and away from my comfort zone.'

Asante's next call-up was too far even for her emboldened mum to drive but it was just as challenging – playing for the newly formed

Under-21s in their first ever tournament, the Nordic Cup. It was not the greatest of starts – England finished bottom of their group and lost on penalties to Norway in the play-off for seventh place in Iceland that July. Asante was undeterred, just as she would be later that summer when a planned soccer scholarship to an American college was scuppered by her semi-professional status. 'I was disappointed but on the back of that lots of good things have happened,' she shrugs in the office at Arsenal's London Colney training ground where the Gunner fulfils her duties as assistant to Clare Wheatley and Arsenal men's chief scout Steve Rowley.

Come September, Asante resumed her politics and English degree at Brunel and her place in the senior England squad, joining up for a friendly in Holland. But it would be the student's last international for a while. The Arsenal player partially tore her anterior cruciate knee ligament in league action in the Gunners' 3-0 home win over Donny Belles on 5 December 2004 and was ruled out for eight weeks. Hard work and more mental strength than the player had ever mustered were key to Asante's rehabilitation. 'I was gutted because it's the worst thing having to watch from the sidelines,' she says. 'And it was real hard work. You work harder getting back than you do when you're fit and in season.' Words of encouragement from her skipper Faye White, who had been there and bought the T-shirt a couple of years previously, helped. 'Faye was giving me advice and support, encouraging me, pushing me through exercises, she was a great help,' says Asante.

Fitting her degree course in with all the recovery work meant she had two timetables to stick to. Asante kept to both. She made it back to win her full debut for England against Northern Ireland in the Algarve Cup and play twenty minutes of Arsenal's 3-0 League Cup final victory over Charlton at Griffin Park. A few weeks later she was joining in Arsenal's League championship celebrations and nine days after her twentieth birthday, Asante made international history. The university student prodded home the only goal at Barnsley's Oakwell Stadium to see a jubilant England record their first ever victory over

Norway, a country with two European titles and a World Cup to its name. Inclusion in Hope Powell's Euro 2005 squad was never guaranteed, but it arrived. Named alongside Asante for the Euro tournament was her Arsenal colleague, the experienced centre-back Mary Phillip.

The veteran defender knew all too well what it was like to make it back into international contention – and to have the Algarve and Norway play a part. Following the birth of her sons Jordan and Marcus, Phillip slipped out of England reckoning. A storming comeback against the Norwegians in the Algarve Cup 2002 gave the then Fulham professional the breakthrough she needed and she has been a mainstay of Powell's England defence ever since. So much so that when Faye White was injured or absent during the World Cup 2007 qualification campaign, Powell looked to the Peckham-based football coach to lead the team on the field. Having lifted the FA Cup in 2003 as Fulham captain in front of 10,389 fans and a television audience of 1.9 million, Phillip was always a candidate for the role, even if she chose to play it down. 'I see myself still as one of the girls, one of the players out there,' she said ahead of the crucial France clash in September 2006. 'When we go out there I wear the captain's armband but we are all captains out on that pitch, we all talk to each other and all drive each other forward.'

Now on the verge of World Cup qualification, England had motored full steam ahead since Phillip and nine of her 2006 international colleagues suffered defeat at the hands of the French in St Etienne four years back. Those World Cup play-off matches had cemented the then Fulham skipper's return to the international fold after a stop-start period of around five years. It had been a welcome return, but not one Phillip says she had desperately hankered after. 'I was in and out, I don't know the reasons, you weren't told,' she says. 'I didn't think anything of it, I just got on with what I was doing.' What Phillip was doing by 2002, was bringing up her two boys and playing professional football for Fulham. It was an easier job than it had been when Phillip had delivered her first son, Jordan, the year of

One match to go! Mary Phillip takes on the captaincy once again for the crucial tie with France.

her World Cup 1995 call-up. Then, the nineteen-year-old had juggled training with matches, motherhood and work as a development coach for Millwall FC.

Millwall's Lionesses were the club Phillip had teamed up with as a teenager following an introduction to the game that began on a gravel pitch inside a London housing estate. But what was initially an after-school flirtation became much more after a chance drive-by recruitment from a youth-club coach. 'I was walking down the road with a friend kicking a ball to each other and a youth worker stopped the car and said, "I run a club would you be able to come?"' she says. The twelve-year-old readily took up the offer once she had cleared it with mum and dad and went from street kickabouts to the midfield hustle and bustle of the Greater London League. Scoring as her underdog Patmore Youth Club side pipped an Arsenal third team to the Anniversary Cup remains one of Phillip's fondest memories of those formative years. As does lifting the cup double she won alongside Katie Chapman with Millwall in 1997.

In Millwall, Phillip had joined a club that had secured an FA Cup success in 1991 and worked their way into the National Division. But when the then midfielder Phillip arrived in the camp not long after that cup triumph, she found weekly thrashings par for the course. 'We had gone through a good few seasons getting battered 8-0, 9-0 by the likes of Doncaster Belles and Arsenal,' Phillip recalls. 'But Jim Hicks worked on our fitness and gave us a level of understanding and the season came and we just clicked together.' Despite the losses, Phillip's command of her new position in the Lionesses' defence was sound enough to win a place in the World Cup 1995 squad. Millwall boss Hicks took time out to put Phillip and Lou Waller through extra fitness training to prepare them for the tournament which would feature Millwall graduate Hope Powell. 'Jim had us up Greenwich Park running and it was bloody hard,' recalls Waller. 'We used to go up the hills, running, doing interval training and stuff like that. I can always remember it because it was so hard.' Phillip never really got the chance to build on that World Cup inclusion, however, as her international career fell away when she learned she was pregnant shortly after the trip to Sweden. It was not the same story domestically.

Despite having given birth to Jordan the season prior to Millwall's silver season, Phillip joined the Chapman twins Sophie and Katie, Lou Waller, Justine Lorton and the rest of the team on the winners' podium in 1997. The laid-back defender had taken pregnancy in her stride and was still donning a training kit and merrily knocking balls into the penalty box for the likes of Lorton to run on to when she was eight months pregnant. Phillip threw herself back into the thick of the action just a few weeks after Jordan arrived. 'That's the nature of the athlete she was and obviously football meant a lot to her,' says Hicks. The sense of camaraderie that knitted the future cup winners together paid dividends whenever her partner or Jordan's grand-parents were not able to step in on away trips. 'I remember Katie and Sophie Chapman playing in their room with him,' she says. 'He would wander off to the rooms and everyone made it easy for me to come back and start playing again.' Hicks played his part too, pacing up and down holding a squawking Jordan in his arms while his team played Everton. 'He was dumped into my arms on the sideline because there was nobody else there,' laughs Hicks. 'So this kid is wailing on the sideline, people are just laughing at me thinking, "What the hell is he going to do with this kid now to placate him?" Oh, it was ridiculous.' Phillip remains impressed at her manager's endeavours even to this day. 'I've got to give him credit,' says Phillip. 'I don't know how he did it.'

And so, when the Millwall girls did the double soon after, it was not just the League and FA cups they held aloft. Toddler Jordan was bounced around on the shoulders of the Lionesses while they celebrated the culmination of all their hard work. 'When we won the cup final, someone took a photo of Sally Ede with him on her shoulders dancing in the changing room,' recalls Phillip. 'I still have that picture.' The image is not the only thing that Phillip has retained from her time at the south London club. She also brought away the much-coveted 'bouncebackability' that footballers speak of during hard times. She says:

> At Millwall we had to work for a good four or five years to get to where we won. The atmosphere that was created when we won was fantastic, I've not been at another club where I've had that satisfaction of losing for so many seasons and then coming up trumps and winning the FA Cup and League Cup. You appreciate it so much more than when you are on a winning run. It builds character, you don't want to lose like that all the time and you are thinking what can we do to get better and the whole team is working at it and then when it comes around and you are winning the FA Cup and League Cup with all the hard work you've put in there you get so much more satisfaction.

Millwall never quite replicated those heady days in the seasons that followed and as the cup-winning team went their various ways, Phillip decided it was time to move on too. The season she gave birth to her second son, Marcus, was the one in which chairman Mohamed Al Fayed had decided to make Fulham professional. By the summer of 2000, Fulham were ready to embark on their first full season as professionals and Millwall stalwart Katie Chapman was leaving to team up with the chairman's side. Hearing that the club were on the lookout for defenders, Phillip put herself forward and Fulham took little persuading. 'Mary was very strong, a strong character, quick, aggressive, a no-nonsense player,' recalls their manager at the time, Frank McMorrow.

Joining up with Al Fayed's sixteen-strong band of professionals at the club's swish training ground at Motspur Park in New Malden, the former Millwall player and teammate Katie Chapman entered a world where drink was banned seventy-two hours before a game and training was a daily requirement. They also found out what it was like to be on the winning end of rugby-score victories such as they had suffered at Millwall. Still in the South East Combination League, Fulham were hitting teams for six, seven, even nineteen that unbeaten season. Phillip fondly recalls the banter of a team who, like the Roman Abramovich-backed Chelsea men's team, were begrudgingly accepted by the rest of the football world because of the success their financial muscle brought. Indeed, Fulham could have adopted the old Millwall adage, 'Everyone hates us and we don't care' during those days. But the down-to-earth Phillip loved those times with Rachel Yankey, Rachel McArthur, Katie Chapman et al regardless. 'They were a great bunch of girls, it was a great atmosphere and we all got on with one another,' she says. 'Finding out how people played, their strengths and weaknesses, you couldn't beat that.'

The mum of two could not better the ease that pervaded her life once she had given up her regular job as development officer with Millwall FC's community sports scheme and assumed the role of professional. Training day in, day out with a ball at your feet was bound to make life easier on the pitch. But being paid to train each day and then being allowed home in the early afternoon with your work completed was a godsend to a busy mother with two young sons as she explains:

> Childcare was easier because I'd finish training and pick Marcus up and have them the whole day, rather than leaving at 9a.m. and getting home at 6p.m. and then having to go training... You are at home at a reasonable time, you're not leaving early in the morning to beat the traffic, you're training at 10a.m. It was a lot easier for me.

Professional status enhanced Phillip's family life, enabling her to enjoy her leisure time shopping, watching films, relaxing with the children in the park and taking them on fun family outings to their favourite theme parks. It did little to bring her in from the cold where England were concerned, however. While fellow Fulhamite Katie Chapman was picked for England's Euro 2001 squad, Phillip did not get a look in. It was not a source of worry as the then twenty-four-year-old was too busy getting on with life. 'Fair play to the girls that were in it,' she says. 'But I wasn't going to sit down and dwell on not being there.'

England may have been put to the back of Phillip's mind during this time, but she was at the forefront of her old World Cup colleague's. Hope Powell brought Phillip back into the fold in 2002, giving the defender a run-out in the Algarve Cup. Packing her bag to join the team in Portugal, Phillip was prepared to meet success or failure with the same stoic attitude she had employed her entire life. 'I was just playing football at another level,' she says. 'I didn't feel any pressure, it was great to be playing for my country but I didn't take any pressure. I take things that are put in front of me and deal with them as they come.' As it turned out, Phillip's calm assurance paid dividends and a strong showing against Norway convinced Powell that she had found the defensive partner for Faye White as England continued their bid to qualify for the World Cup. By that season's end, Phillip had repeated her FA and League cup trick, this time with Fulham. She was not about to repeat her feat of landing a place at the World Cup, however. Phillip was one of the emotionally and physically drained England players who collapsed on to the turf in St Etienne having lost out on the fifth European spot to France amid the caterwauls of the home nation's supporters.

It was a loss that marked a sea change in the England squad that Phillip recognised by the time she was set to win her fiftieth cap and lead her country out against France in September 2006. Speaking ahead of the trip to Rennes, Phillip was frank in her assessment of the England she had come to know:

> I think the team now has got a lot more backing. We are more tooled up going into this game. We were already 1-0 down from the home game [in 2002] so we were going out there and looking to score two goals to literally go through which was a bit of a task for us. This time round it's all level and we're looking just to go out there for the win.

Phillip was an Arsenal player by the time of this France encounter, having left Fulham with five major titles the season after they reverted back to semi-professional status. Returning to life in football development amid the grass roots, the Level Three-qualified coach understood the importance of success in France. 'It's the biggest growing sport in the country and for us to get to the World Cup will pick the game up that bit more,' she said. 'The way we've been playing, we're not going to be looking for any kind of draw. We are going to go out there full attack.'

And so England did, with Kelly Smith and Karen Carney setting their sights on Sarah Bouhaddi's goal within minutes of running out at the imposing Stade de la Route de Lorient in front of 19,215 fans and a live BBC3 audience on 30 September 2006. France craves victory tonight as much as England, though, and it shows as Laëtitia Tonazzi nips past Rachel Unitt to put in a shot but it goes well over. The duel between Marinette Pichon and Rachel Brown that was such a feature in the previous meeting resumes, the striker testing the keeper with two rapid shots. Hoda Lattaf half-volleys strongly in the fortieth minute but once again, Brown smothers the ball. England are on the back foot just before the break, with Unitt suffering an ankle injury. The defender's game is over but England have the capable Casey Stoney to fall back on.

The entire defence need their wits about them as France take the initiative after the break with the unmarked Sandrine Soubeyrand just failing to get onto the end of a deep Sonia Bompastor free-kick. Pichon piles on the pressure, forcing another good save from Brown, but England get the breakthrough on sixty-three minutes when a wonderful Rachel Yankey free-kick from the right is put past Bouhaddi by Hoda Lattaf under pressure from Fara Williams. England scream and punch the air with relief, the squad descend on Williams, the few hundred England fans and players' families in the upper tier of the Tribune Ville de Rennes stand erupt and Sue Smith bangs her head on the dugout after leaping off the bench in jubilation. It is marked down as an own goal but Williams is having none of it. 'I'm claiming that goal, it hit my shoulder,' she says. 'It means everything to me even though it wasn't given to me.' There are twenty-seven minutes on the clock remaining but to the England players it feels like an eternity as they run euphorically but with heavy legs back to the centre circle. 'I was more tired after scoring than before,' says Williams. 'You are waiting for the end of the game but it dragged. Kelly Smith said to me, "I'm shattered" and that was just after the goal. It was the hardest thing ever.' England know they cannot take their foot off the pedal but Anita Asante calmly deals with everything that is thrown at her while at the other end Eniola Aluko shrugs off her marker and powers towards the goal but shoots over. Fresh legs arrive in the form of Sue Smith as she is thrown on for Rachel Yankey with twelve minutes remaining and frantically checking the stadium clock, England know they need to hang on for just a few more minutes. Then France substitute Ludivine Diguelman knocks an up-and-under from the left that loops over

Joy, relief and celebration for Hope Powell at the end of a tough but successful qualification campaign.

Brown and into the far top corner of the goal. This time the stadium erupts and the entire France team go wild, racing over to the bench as if their jobs are done. 'It was a cross, I stepped to attack it and then misjudged it,' says Brown. 'But my reaction was they are not going to score again, it's alright, and that's the attitude we created among ourselves.' France must score again, though, as a draw will not do if they are to go through and the players are soon sent packing back to the centre circle to chase another goal. But it is England who have their tails up and Bouhaddi's mistake in the final minute sees Aluko side-foot towards an empty net from the edge of the area. The shot hits the post but it does not matter, referee Jenny Palmqvist blows for full-time and England are into the World Cup for the first time in twelve years. Faye White, commentating for BBC3, is almost speechless and rushes out of the studio and on to the pitch as fast as her crutches will carry her. Kelly Smith dances a jig of delight before putting a comforting arm around the shoulders of Pichon, her old teammate from Philadelphia Charge. Trevor Brooking checks on Sue Smith's sore head and the handful of British journalists in the press tribune rush to congratulate the players and grab a few choice quotes.

Back in the changing rooms, the celebrations continue as everyone is called up to dance in the centre of the tiled floor, including the FA's media manager who jumps onto the treatment table and jives with joy. In the aftermath Powell says:

> We knew it was always going to be tight. You know, we dug deep, everybody dug deep right until the end and it's tremendous. I'm so happy for them. I think they're exhausted. The most important thing is we must enjoy this. We must appreciate what we've done. Let's enjoy it, let's relish the moment. We deserve to.

Meet the Players

ENIOLA ALUKO

DATE OF BIRTH: 21 February 1987

CLUBS: Birmingham City, Charlton Athletic

ENGLAND DEBUT: 18 September 2004, Netherlands 1–2 England at Heerhugowaard, Netherlands

ANITA ASANTE

DATE OF BIRTH: 27 April 1985

CLUBS: Arsenal

ENGLAND DEBUT: 14 May 2004, England 1–0 Iceland at Peterborough

AMANDA BARR

DATE OF BIRTH: 2 May 1982

CLUBS: Stockport County, Everton, Doncaster Belles, Everton, Charlton Athletic, Birmingham City, Charlton Athletic, Blackburn Rovers, Leeds United

ENGLAND DEBUT: 27 May 2001, England 1-0 Scotland at Bolton

RACHEL BROWN

DATE OF BIRTH: 2 July 1980

CLUBS: Accrington Stanley, Liverpool, University of Alabama (USA), University of Pittsburgh (USA), Everton, ÍBV (Iceland), Everton

ENGLAND DEBUT: 27 February 1997, England 4-6 Germany at Preston.

KAREN CARNEY

DATE OF BIRTH: 1 August 1987

CLUBS: Birmingham City, Arsenal

ENGLAND DEBUT: 17 February 2005, England 4-1 Italy at Milton Keynes

SIOBHAN CHAMBERLAIN

DATE OF BIRTH: 15 August 1983

CLUBS: Chelsea, Fulham, Birmingham City, Bristol Academy

ENGLAND DEBUT: 22 September 2004, Netherlands 0-1 England at Tuitjenhorn, Netherlands

KATIE CHAPMAN

DATE OF BIRTH: 15 June 1982

CLUBS: Millwall Lionesses, Fulham, Charlton Athletic, Arsenal

ENGLAND DEBUT: 13 May 2000, England 1-0 Switzerland at Bristol

VICKY EXLEY

DATE OF BIRTH: 22 October 1975

CLUBS: Sheffield Wednesday, Doncaster Belles

ENGLAND DEBUT: 16 March 1996, Italy 2-1 England at Cosenza, Italy

JODY HANDLEY

DATE OF BIRTH: 12 March 1979

CLUBS: Wolverhampton Wanderers, Liverpool, Everton, Doncaster Belles, Everton

ENGLAND DEBUT: 23 July 2002, England 0-1 Nigeria at Norwich

LINDSAY JOHNSON

DATE OF BIRTH: 8 May 1980

CLUBS: Liverpool, Everton

ENGLAND DEBUT: 18 September 2004, Netherlands 1-2 England at Heerhugowaard, Netherlands

MARY PHILLIP

DATE OF BIRTH: 14 March 1977

CLUBS: Millwall Lionesses, Fulham, Arsenal

ENGLAND DEBUT: 18 April 1996, Croatia 0-2 England at Osijek, Croatia

JO POTTER

DATE OF BIRTH: 13 November 1984

CLUBS: Birmingham City, Arsenal, Birmingham City, Charlton Athletic

ENGLAND DEBUT: 18 September 2004, Netherlands 1-2 England at Heerhugowaard, Netherlands

LIANNE SANDERSON

DATE OF BIRTH: 3 February 1988

CLUBS: Arsenal

ENGLAND DEBUT: 11 May 2006, England 2-0 Hungary at Southampton

ALEX SCOTT

DATE OF BIRTH: 14 October 1984

CLUBS: Arsenal, Birmingham City, Arsenal

ENGLAND DEBUT: 18 September 2004, Netherlands 1-2 England at Heerhugowaard, Netherlands

JILL SCOTT

DATE OF BIRTH: 2 February 1987

CLUBS: Sunderland, Everton

ENGLAND DEBUT: 31 August 2006, England 4-0 Netherlands at Charlton

KELLY SMITH

DATE OF BIRTH: 29 October 1978

CLUBS: Wembley, Arsenal, Seton Hall University (USA), New Jersey Lady Stallions (USA), Philadelphia Charge (USA), New Jersey Wildcats (USA), Arsenal

ENGLAND DEBUT: 1 November 1995, England 1-1 Italy at Sunderland

SUE SMITH

DATE OF BIRTH: 24 November 1979

CLUBS: Tranmere Rovers, Leeds United

ENGLAND DEBUT: 27 February 1997, England 4-6 Germany at Preston